GODDESS

AT HOME

ROCKPORT

GLOUCESTER MASSACHUSETTS

GODDESS AT HOME

ROCKPORT PUBLISHERS

DIVINE INTERIORS INSPIRED BY

*Aphrodite, Artemis, Athena, Demeter,
Hera, Hestia & Persephone*

A. BRONWYN LLEWELLYN

First published in the United States of America by

Rockport Publishers, Inc.

33 Commercial Street

Gloucester, Massachusetts 01930-5089

Telephone: (978) 282-9590

Fax: (978) 283-2742

www.rockpub.com

Library of Congress Cataloging-in-Publication Data

Llewellyn, A. Bronwyn (Anita Bronwyn)

    Goddess at home : divine interiors inspired by Aphrodite, Artemis, Athena, Demeter, Hera, Hestia, and Persephone / A. Bronwyn Llewellyn.

        p.   cm.

   ISBN 1-56496-920-7

   1. Interior decoration-Psychological aspects. 2. Goddesses (Greek)—Miscellanea. I. Title.

NK2113 .L62 2003

747'.082—dc21   2002011365

10 9 8 7 6 5 4 3 2 1

Cover Design: Wherefore Art?

Design: Wherefore Art?

Layout & Production: Leeann Leftwich Zajas

Cover Image: Villa Vallombrosa in Whitley Heights. Designed by architect Nathan Coleman, a typical Spanish Colonial Revival development from the 1920s, now a National Historical Monument and the home of Photographer Tim Street-Porter and Interior Designer Annie Kelly.

Back Cover Image: Copyright Réunion des Musées Nationaux/Art Resource, NY

Project Manager/Copyeditor: Stacey Ann Follin

Proofreader: Beth Pitcher

Printed in China

To Carolyn, Edeen, Joan, Kathryn, Meera, Paula, and Rachel.

They're all goddesses!

CONTENTS

8   Introduction

10   Aphrodite: Goddess of Love, Passion & Beauty

34   Artemis: Goddess of the Hunt, Nature & Independence

52   Athena: Goddess of Wisdom, Civilization & the Arts

70   Demeter: Goddess of the Harvest & Fertility

88   Hera: Goddess of Marriage

106   Hestia: Goddess of Hearth & Home

124   Persephone: Goddess of Life, Renewal & Transformation

138   Photographer credits

141   Resources

143   Acknowledgments

144   About the Author

What lies behind us and what lies before us are tiny matters,
compared to what lies within us.

—RALPH WALDO EMERSON

INTRODUCTION

IF EVERY MAN IS KING OF HIS CASTLE, EVERY WOMAN SHOULD BE GODDESS OF HER HOME. CALL ON THE SPIRIT OF THE SEVEN ANCIENT GREEK GODDESSES—APHRODITE, ARTEMIS, ATHENA, DEMETER, HERA, HESTIA, AND PERSEPHONE—AND YOU CAN INFUSE YOUR HOME WITH A DIVINE GRACE AND BEAUTY WORTHY OF THE GODDESS IN YOU.

Just as the Greeks welcomed the goddesses into every aspect of their lives, you can welcome them into your home—and transform your life in the process. Intentionally or not, your dwelling speaks volumes about you. Let these seven goddesses help you fashion living spaces that uniquely reflect you, in much the same way they've been called on in recent years to help women nourish ambitions and fulfill dreams. With their guidance, you can turn the rooms in your home into havens that enhance your strengths and encourage those qualities you wish to nurture in yourself.

Each goddess has long been associated with particular colors, animals, plants, seasons, and objects. Infinite ways to incorporate each goddess into your rooms abound—for example, by adding specific objects or using colors, patterns, or motifs redolent of her themes. The Victorians infused bouquets of flowers with symbolic messages, depending on the type of flowers and their arrangement. Similarly, the goddesses can add depth and meaning to your surroundings, even if you're the only one who can decipher the significance hidden there. When the symbols take tangible and familiar form, such as keeping a small figure of an owl in your office or lighting a candle to Hestia, they remind you of their meaning every time you look at them. A sheaf of wheat becomes not merely an adornment for your kitchen but a homage to the great Demeter's gift of bountiful crops. Look closely at each goddess, and you'll glimpse the interconnectedness of all living things, the humor and fallibility of human beings, and the greatness and promise that reside within each of us.

Scholars believe the major Greek goddesses are individual characteristics long ago splintered from one or two even-more-powerful goddesses. Within every woman, there are fragments of each of these goddesses, to a greater or lesser degree. For you, one or two will predominate over the others, and they may change at various times in your life. As I worked on this book, I realized that I had accented my home with the four goddesses that resonate for me. My living room combines Hestia, with its chairs grouped cozily around the often-used fireplace and a mantel adorned with candles, with Artemis in the leaf-patterned carpet, vines curling over the windows, and the gray-green walls subtle as a dusky glade. Demeter reigns in my kitchen, where the faces of my friends' children adorn the refrigerator and the vanilla enamel molding and cabinetry look good enough eat. A small bronze bust of Athena watches over my computer, and a beautiful gold and blue rug reminds me of her artistry. My father's photograph rests atop his piano, which I inherited. As I come to appreciate Aphrodite, Hera, and Persephone, I'm adding the notes of their voices as well. And I'm keeping my eyes peeled for that perfect throne for the dining room.

Although you won't find specific instructions on upholstering or painting techniques in *Goddess at Home*, you'll find plenty of inspiration in these stunningly beautiful interiors. Ideas nurture creativity, so embrace, interpret, and make them your own. How to incorporate them into your rooms is up to you and your imagination. Outfit one room or every room to honor the private goddesses that represent your desires, ambitions, values, and dreams. Goddess in the bedroom? With a little help from Aphrodite, you can transform a room of sleep into a boudoir of passionate excess. Goddess in the dining room? Look to queenly Hera to help you reign supreme in your domicile. Just remember: What matters is that the result holds meaning for you and brings you pleasure.

You *are* the goddess at home. Just as the ancient myths wove together old stories imperfectly but to great effect, so you can assemble the motifs of these beautiful and meaningful deities. Make the goddess whole again by reuniting all her different aspects. Make all the goddesses your own—and bring them home.

Embrace the Goddess and her divine perception of you. Ask her to reveal to you the you she has in mind.

—MARIANNE WILLIAMSON

What is life, what is joy without golden Aphrodite?
May I die when these things no longer move me—hidden love affairs, sweet nothings, and bed.
— MIMNERMUS OF COLOPHON

APHRODITE
GODDESS OF LOVE, PASSION & BEAUTY

AS THE EPITOME OF LOVELINESS AND THE GODDESS OF TENDER PASSIONS, APHRODITE CAUSED LOVE TO BLOOM IN THE HEARTS OF MAN AND BEAST ALIKE. HER VOLUPTUOUS FORM BESPEAKS ALL THAT IS BEAUTIFUL, FROM CLASSICAL GREECE TO TODAY'S TECHNOLOGICAL AGE. THE ROMANS MELDED HER LORE WITH THAT OF VENUS, A SIMPLER GODDESS OF YOUTHFUL FLIRTATIONS, AND NOW THEY INTERMINGLE AS SYNONYMS FOR *LOVE*.

Some legends say Aphrodite was a daughter of Zeus. An older tale describes how Cronos plotted with his mother Gaea to castrate his father Uranus, and tossed the sky god's genitals into the sea. Out of the reddened, frothy waves emerged the golden-haired Aphrodite atop a scallop shell, saltwater dripping as pearls to her dainty feet. Everywhere she went, grass grew, birds sang, and love flourished.

It's apt that the goddess of love should have many lovers; indeed, gods and mortal men alike found her sensuality irresistible. Even though she proudly disdained any permanent union, Zeus gave her in marriage to the homely blacksmith Hephaestus, who crafted thunderbolts for the Olympian ruler. But Aphrodite's charms proved too powerful to be confined and, unfortunately for her husband, she shared them liberally.

One of Aphrodite's most famous liaisons was with Ares, the god of war and her husband's brother. Told of their affair by Helios, the cuckolded blacksmith wrought a net of gold so fine it was invisible. This he fastened over the bed to catch the lovers in their tryst.

Aphrodite's uninhibited libido distinguishes her from other Greek deities, whose domains and exploits ranged far and wide. She alone ruled over the sweep of human passion. Anyone who dared disrupt the natural course of love felt her wrath, and she rewarded those who succumbed to their lusty appetites. Aphrodite is sometimes thought of as the "alchemical" goddess, for when we're in love, we change, and certainly "chemistry" has everything to do with love. She submits to no power—certainly not within her realm of love. She remains her own woman.

The goddess Aphrodite is associated with everything relating to the senses. She surrounds herself with beauty and finds beauty in whatever she beholds. In love and in life, her one special gift is rejoicing in the moment: Each new love is as fresh and innocent as the first; every experience deserves passionate attention. Anyone seeking to emulate her would do well to follow this philosophy in all endeavors.

In the Judgment of Paris, Aphrodite won the golden apple when she was named more beautiful than either Hera or Athena. In truth, she needed no one to judge her beauty for she remained serene in her self-knowledge, fully aware of her unique inner strengths. In art, she's usually shown unclothed, whether rising provocatively from the sea or reclining to gaze calmly at the viewer, because she's supremely comfortable with her own body.

APHRODITE IN YOUR BEDROOM

THROUGHOUT HISTORY, THE APHRODITE WOMAN HAS TAKEN MANY NAMES AND FORMS—VENUS, EVE, SALOME, CLEOPATRA, CAMILLE, ANNA KARENINA, JOSEPHINE, JEAN HARLOW, MARILYN MONROE, GRETA GARBO, ELIZABETH TAYLOR, SOPHIA LOREN, AND NOW YOU. LET APHRODITE WORK HER MAGIC IN YOUR BOUDOIR AND BATH BY CALLING UPON THE SYMBOLS, COLORS, AND HALLMARKS OF HER SENSUOUS SPIRIT.

What surroundings make you feel as though you're falling in love? When the senses reach fever pitch, creativity sparkles and all things are possible. The bedroom is the intimate and mysterious place where we sleep, dream, and make love. Aphrodite's bedroom is a sensual cocoon, one in which to luxuriate without guilt. Here you can come to relax, rejuvenate, and be yourself. Banish Athena's concerns about work and Demeter's attention to family and make this one room a temple to your own feminine gifts. Keep Aphrodite's realm a serene haven for love and indulgence.

Someone once said that allure is half attitude and the rest theater. If that is true, Aphrodite's bedroom sets the stage for any plays of passion you contrive. Give this room over to the senses. Mask the outside world with sounds of water, music, or wind chimes. Mix different fabrics—linen and lace, silk and velvet, sheers and cashmere, suede and linen, cotton and fur. For inspiration, keep a book of love poems or dream interpretations on the nightstand. Record your thoughts and dreams in a journal. Embroider a love sonnet on a pillowcase, or paint it as a frieze near the ceiling.

THE SYMBOLS OF LOVE

Dolphins

Doves

Gold—in accessories, cords, fabrics, furniture

Sparrows

Stars (Remember: Venus is the morning star.)

Swans

Wrought iron and other metals in the husband's honor

THE COLORS OF PASSION

Hues of the sea—blues, greens, and pearly whites

Pinks

Purples

Reds

THE HALLMARKS OF BEAUTY

Apples or other ripe, sweet fruit

Fragrance—especially myrtle and myrrh

Flowers—particularly the rose and the red anemone

Mirrors

Shells—particularly the scallop shell

Wild strawberries

Aphrodite's bedroom is part boudoir, part sanctuary. Pay homage to beauty at a sensuous dressing table. Layer pink hues for drama and depth. Indulge your toes with a soft carpet. Golden accessories hint at love's riches.

Just being in a room with myself is almost more stimulation than I can bear.

—KATE BRAVERMAN

At Aphrodite's birth, the rose first appeared, and thereafter she was known as the goddess of flowers. To this day, flowers remain inextricably linked with love. When we're in love, we bloom. Cleopatra seduced Antony knee-deep in rose petals, so use sumptuous flower patterns in carpets, wallpaper, textiles, and art. Decorate the bedposts with garlands. Perfume the air with jasmine-scented candles and fresh bouquets. Spray a delicate scent beneath the pillows.

If a life without passion is colorless, the reverse is surely true. Red not only symbolizes passion, fervor, and magic, just looking at it causes the heart to race and blood pressure to rise. Run the gamut of red from softest pink to richest ruby, or choose one shade and layer it in different materials: ceramic, chintz, stone, wool, and roses. Crimson anemones sprouted from the blood of Aphrodite's beloved Adonis. Festoon your bedroom with dramatic blossoms. Pale blue and turquoise are restful watery colors for Aphrodite's bedroom. Paint the ceiling the color of an Aegean sky. Plunge into the abyssal depths or nighttime with deep midnight blue. Paint the trim a creamy white, the color of stars or the inside of a nautilus shell.

You can find inspiration whether you prefer Art Deco or Rococo, techno-modern or flea-market chic. Just add a bit of Aphrodite's spirit to whatever your style and budget, and summon the goddess.

In the bedroom, sleep and dreams wax and wane like the ocean tides of Aphrodite's birthplace. Splurge on luxurious bedding that encourages romance as well as blissful sleep. Adorn your love nest with pillows soft as swan's down, and pile up satiny comforters. Keep the outside world at bay with padded and fabric-wrapped wall panels mounted to muffle noise. Drape mosquito netting or curtains around the bed for privacy.

Acknowledge the blacksmithing talents of Aphrodite's husband with a finely wrought metal bed, dressing table, or chair embellished with swans, shells, or another one of Aphrodite's sacred motifs. Devise your own delicate trap for dreams or a lover by draping the bed with gold-colored gauze.

LEFT: Add notes of purple passion, golden glamour, enchantment, outrageousness, voluptuous pattern, and deep comfort. There is no yesterday or tomorrow in Aphrodite's bedroom, only now. Make that "now" a romantic, exotic adventure.

OPPOSITE: Escape to realms of Aphrodite's sensuous deep. Curl up in plump, soft satin pillows the color of rich cream, lose yourself in the cool aquamarines of the sea, and take a nap—or something more libidinous.

I believe that everything in one's house should be comfortable,
but one's bedroom must be more than comfortable: It must be intimate.

—ELSIE DE WOLFE

Sights, sounds, smells, and textures affect one another when juxtaposed. Select one or two of Aphrodite's motifs and colors to complement the bedroom and bath. Change the accessories with the seasons.

The delicate scallop shell is a symbol of Aphrodite's beauty. Find shell motifs on furniture, textiles, lamps, ceramics, or rugs. Display a collection or one beautiful shell on a table. Pile several large ones in a wicker chair or basket.

Myrrh is sacred to Aphrodite. Dried myrrh adds a woody accent to potpourri. Include live branches in bouquets. Aphrodite draped herself with myrtle to hide from the satyrs, and the plant grew near her sacred temples. Add its spicy orange fragrance to an herb-filled pillow to beckon a goddess' dreams.

Artists depict this goddess' chariot drawn by swans or doves. Find ways to incorporate their images in the bedroom. Sparrows and geese are also associated with this goddess.

Knot golden cord to tie back draperies and connote the "ties of love." Or use it as piping on a duvet.

Wild strawberries and pinecones are sacred to the Roman goddess Venus. Hang botanical prints with their images in the bedroom.

Aphrodite is sometimes depicted admiring her beauty in a mirror. Include an ornate or elegant mirror over a dressing table or a chest of drawers, or allow it to be freestanding.

What could be more inviting than tea for two in a bed of bowers, blessed by Cupid himself, and dressed in fine white linens. Create your own love nest with slender birch branches, silk flowers, ivy, ribbon, and grapevine.

I think we dream so we don't have to be apart so long.
If we're in each other's dreams, we can be together all the time.
—THOMAS HOBBES

The burnished metallic swirls of a baroque headboard echo the Italianate elegance of the bedroom. Golden pillows, delicate furniture, and antique artwork summon Venetian—and Venusian—dreams.

The story of Pygmalion tells how he fell in love with an ivory likeness of Aphrodite. She eventually took pity on him and breathed life into the cold statue so that he might have the object of his affection. Pygmalion's dream not only came true but also came to life, thanks to the Goddess of Love.

Breathe a little life into your bedroom, and embrace the sensations that Aphrodite stirs—and your dreams may come true, too. Don't be intimidated by her intense sexuality. Borrow some of Aphrodite's self-confidence, and create a room that is a little out of the ordinary for you. Don't limit yourself—Aphrodite wouldn't. Experiment. Explore. Excite.

You don't think of yourself as a wanton sex goddess? Think again. Even if you feel much more at home in Athena's power-charged workspace or Demeter's comfortable kitchen, you can benefit from Aphrodite's influence. Start small. Bedeck a silk pillow with luscious tassels and braids, prominently display a small exquisite sculpture, or paint one wall a hue that "warmeth the blood." Beautiful objects and colors can lift a commonplace room from routine to resplendent—and lift you right along with them.

Entertain a lover, or dreams of one,
in a comfortable chaise overlooking
a beautiful tromp l'oeil ocean view.

Beauty satisfies the senses completely and at the same time uplifts the soul.

—FRANZ GRILLPARZER

ABOVE: Flowers cascade around whimsical swans on an 18th-century French Aubusson carpet fit for Aphrodite's boudoir.

LEFT: The perfect stone vase. An antique chaise longue. A trio of elegant prints. Touches like these add grace and beauty to any Aphrodite's bedroom. And a sensuous nude sculpture doesn't hurt, either.

Lift your bed high off the ground to create a love nest worthy of Aphrodite herself.

There is a reason why lovers present chocolate and roses to their paramours—their rich taste and aroma awaken the senses. You, too, can find new and unexpected ways to enhance sensual enjoyment in your own boudoir.

Take your inspiration from Aphrodites throughout history. In medieval times, women perfumed their skin with essences of rose, orange, and myrtle to tempt their lovers. Josephine Baker relied on Jean Patou's Joy, Mae West on Rochas' Femme, Rita Hayworth on Guerlain's Shalimar.

Sarah Bernhardt and her companion of the moment dined on truffles and Bordeaux while reclining on opulent carpets festooned with blossoms. Marilyn Monroe preferred champagne and cherry tomatoes stuffed with cream cheese and caviar served unadorned and undressed in an unmade bed.

Which brings us to the importance of linens. Dress Aphrodite's bed as you would an empress, with feathery down and gorgeous linens in the highest thread count you can afford. The difference is palpable, when the fabrics smooth over your body like a creamy lotion. Whether glossy satin, real linen, or Egyptian cotton, adorned with flowers or rich damask patterns, wrap them around you like a lover's embrace. Who needs a nightgown?

Aphrodite is a blazing star in the heavenly galaxy of goddesses, so it's no surprise that the stars themselves are associated with her. The Greeks worshipped her as Urania, "heavenly one," and the Romans christened her Venus, silvery star of morning and evening. Bedazzle your admirers by bringing the romance of starlight into your bedroom. Paint your ceiling a midnight blue, and scatter glittering stars across it. Or install a skylight, and let the magic of true stardust twinkle down on your boudoir. Even a sparkling night-light can evoke the starry sex appeal of the Goddess of Love.

Cast your cares away on crisp
cotton waves of Aegean blue and
freshwater pearl, as Aphrodite's son
takes aim with his arrows of love.

Venus herself would feel at home in Marie Antoinette's boudoir at Château de Fontainebleau, with its rich mahogany underfoot and neoclassical wood, stucco, and gold decor. More is more in a bedroom fit for a queen.

Sometimes the lightest touch is the best, as Aphrodite well knew. In this serene back-to-nature space, a gold-framed mirror adds a touch of the goddess, as do the pearly white tulips.

With Aphrodite, the stars reach from the heavens above to the seas below. With a starfish motif, you can call on Aphrodite's astral and aquatic connections. Fill an antique aquarium with seashells, smooth pebbles, or a few lavender-scented candles. Larger shells can serve as wall sconces, candleholders, or bowls for potpourri.

Remember that lovers see the world through rose-colored glasses. Layer sheer lipstick–colored fabrics at the window for a shimmering romantic effect that changes with the light and the whispering breeze. Antique bottles on a sun-filled shelf cast crystalline shadows of garnet, rose, and gold over pale walls. Flowers fill the air with fragrance—and set the stage for amorous adventures.

When Hephaestus crafted the first woman, it was Aphrodite who bestowed on her the radiant beauty and desirability that made her utterly irresistible to men—to their woe. Pandora's curiosity, they say, unleashed all the troubles of the world—not the least of which were the entanglements of love. Unpredictable love, whose pains bring a quickening breath and indescribable joy, dissolves memory of time before Cupid's arrow struck.

What cares Aphrodite's devotee if no lover comes to call? Assuage the pangs of unrequited love with the luxurious beauty of your own pleasure dome. The Goddess of Love reminds us that other lovers will always share her realm. This paean to her glories remains for your enjoyment whenever you desire.

APHRODITE IN YOUR BATH

Famously depicted emerging naked from the sea, coy-eyed Aphrodite floated demurely to Cyprus in a scallop shell. Even her name means "foam-born," so closely tied to the sea is this goddess. Find ways to bring the ocean, its scents and sensibility, into Aphrodite's bath through color, fragrance, texture, and motif.

Sea-foam green, aquamarine, the ocean at dawn—use these and other colors that remind you of the sea to evoke Aphrodite's aquatic origins. Decorate the bathroom to resemble an undersea grotto, complete with flooring the color of kelp or worn pebbles. Paint the walls the color of goldfish, sea grass, or coral. Use accents in hues of dunes, whitecaps, or sand dollars. Faux paint details to resemble tortoiseshell, a brilliant coral reef, or the nacreous pink heart of a seashell. Sew tiny seashells onto muslin as a curtain for window or shower.

Each spring the Three Graces renewed Aphrodite in ritual ablutions of saltwater and immortal oils. You can find your spiritual transformation in a long, pampering bath. Restore and rejuvenate your soul in a deep stone tub. Massage away the day's cares with aromatic lotions and essential oils from graceful flagons. Take a lesson from the oyster in how to deal with life's little irritations. Slow down in the gleam of candlelight. Set cares adrift on waves of soft music or ocean sounds. Dream of pearls where once there were grains of sand.

Give a prominent place to a piece of
sculpture, photograph, or other
artwork that celebrates the beauty
of the human body.

EVOKING APHRODITE IN THE BATH

- Adorn Aphrodite's watery retreat with gold-toned fixtures in the shape of graceful swans.

- Hang an image of the sea or beach, or a scattering of vintage seaside postcards in pretty frames.

- Display shells, smooth stones, a chunk of coral, or other beach treasures, or place a few on the edge of the tub or in the shower. Use a large shell for soaps and other toiletries.

- Keep velvety towels in a basket woven out of dried seaweed.

- Choose bath salts, oils, bubbles, candles, and lotions that smell of sea spray and flower petals.

- Natural loofahs and wooden brushes and combs ritualize your baths.

- Water may not drip as pearls from your toes as it did from Aphrodite's but you can still pamper your feet with thick cotton rugs. Tie back the shower curtain with loops of fake pearls or drip them from light fixtures.

- Mirrors signify the mind, the soul, truth, and self-knowledge. Admire your own goddess beauty in a mirror framed with shells or burnished gold-toned wood, elaborately carved or coolly modern.

- Remember the playfulness of this goddess with an image or small figure of a dolphin, an animal sacred to Aphrodite. Decorate the walls with hand-painted tiles or bas-reliefs of shells, fish, or other sea creatures.

I have bathed in the poem of the sea...
devouring the green azures.

—ARTHUR RIMBAUD

In a colorfully tiled shower big enough for two, drench yourself in the cool waters of the very sea that gave birth to Aphrodite in all her womanly glory.

Aphrodite's love, Nerites, was said to be the fairest of any man or god. Together they lived in the sea until the goddess of love was to be granted a place in the pantheon of Olympians. She entreated Nerites to accompany her, but he preferred to stay in the sea, so Aphrodite turned him into a beautiful cockle.

Bring a love goddess' sea change to your bath. Hang long strands of tiny shells as a curtain and mimic light's dappling play over a rocky inlet. Wire smooth shards of beach glass into sun catchers that dance over tiles the color of sand dunes, and add a rug soft as lapping waves. Contemplate a sculptural piece of tide-worn driftwood. Loop raffia through a muslin shower curtain, and adorn it with dried starfish or sand dollars. Assemble small pieces of weathered wood into a frame for a mirror, and admire your likeness in Aphrodite's abode.

Transform your bathing space into the retreat you deserve—and then retreat there as often as you can. If Jayne Mansfield could bathe in pink champagne twice a week, you can scatter blushing rose petals and a bit of rose oil in a warm bath. Or disappear into a cloud of bubbles until your tootsies wrinkle. Give in to these moments utterly and completely. Let Aphrodite lead you to your serene sensual self.

ABOVE: Honor the female face of the goddess, and launch a thousand ships of your own.

OPPOSITE: With its chic neoclassic appointments—the graceful lighting, the leaded scrolled windows, the enclosed porcelain tub, the goddess bust—this elegant space welcomes bathing beauties of all ages.

LEFT: Picture Cleopatra in this exotic space, surrounded by fern, ivy, and gray silk. Design your own bathing hideaway in the style of your favorite Aphrodite archetype.

My bounty is as boundless as the sea, My love as deep; the more I give to thee, The more I have, for both are infinite.

—JULIET

Aphrodite understood the art of self-indulgence. Whether combing her hair or bathing her body, she devoted herself completely to her own sensual fulfillment. You can do the same—and you should! Make it easy to be good to yourself; stock up on bubble bath, aromatic lotions, exotic soaps, and fluffy towels.

But, remember, in the world according to Aphrodite, bathrooms aren't just for bathing and grooming. Bathrooms are an extension of the bedroom, as lust is an extension of love. Think Susan Sarandon and Kevin Costner in *Bull Durham*, sloshing around together in the tub surrounded by a hundred burning candles; Dennis Quaid and Ellen Barkin in *The Big Easy*, turning teeth brushing into an erotic event. Then, think of you and yours in your own bathing space, doing your thing.

Be prepared for spontaneous escapades. Indulge in a big sunken tub, a big stall with dual shower heads, or both. Add a big chair or chaise for impromptu mutual manicures and massages. Deck your aphrodisiac bath with the tools you'll need to work your goddess magic—scented candles, flowers, and chilled champagne flutes. Pile bath trays with soaps, shampoos, and loofahs for his-and-her grooming. (Remember Robert Redford washing Meryl Streep's hair in *Out of Africa*?) Position a waterproof radio or CD player within arm's reach for easy mood music. And don't forget the matching thick terry robes.

Drifting daisies invite playful intimacy in the bath, and rippling sea green glass provides the privacy discretion dictates.

ABOVE: Fill your bathing space with all of the necessary luxuries that invite the pampering of body and soul—sea salts, soft white towels, a hint of lavender. For luck in love, add an image of the Aphrodite icon of your choice—like the Marilyn print here.

OPPOSITE: Place a beautiful tub big enough for two center stage in a bathing space, and let nature takes its course—with a little help from Aphrodite, of course.

The rude sea grew civil at her song, And certain stars shot madly from their spheres To hear the sea-maid's music.

— SHAKESPEARE

Nature never did betray the heart that loved her.

—WILLIAM WORDSWORTH

ARTEMIS
GODDESS OF THE HUNT, NATURE & INDEPENDENCE

ARTEMIS WAS THE MOST WELL-LOVED GODDESS IN ANCIENT GREECE, ABOVE APHRODITE, ATHENA, OR DEMETER, AND PARTICULARLY BELOVED BY WOMEN. ALTHOUGH SHE IS COMMONLY THOUGHT OF AS THE GODDESS OF THE HUNT, IN TRUTH HER LORE IS COMPLEX, AND HER MEANING MORE ANCIENT AND SUGGESTIVE.

In myth, Artemis, goddess of the moon, is the twin of Apollo, god of the sun, and the child of Zeus's relationship with Leto. In a jealous rage Zeus's wife, Hera, sent a serpent after the pregnant goddess, but newborn Artemis protected her mother and helped her give birth to Apollo. Thus she acquired the bearing of children in her domain, and in ancient Greece women prayed to her for painless labor and delivery.

When Artemis was a young girl, she asked Zeus not for jewelry or other trappings of girlhood, but for only those items that would assure her independence and feed her spirit of adventure. She sought eternal virginity, a bow and arrows like Apollo's, a saffron and red hunting tunic that fell only to her knees so that she could run freely, nymphs to accompany her, and the "office of bringing light." Zeus was delighted to grant these gifts to his precocious child, and added thirty cities and all their roads and harbors to her guardianship. For her use, the Cyclops crafted a silver bow curved like the crescent moon and a quiver of arrows honed to razor sharpness.

As one of the virgin goddesses with Athena and Hestia, Artemis is never described in sexual liaisons with gods or mortal men. Indeed, any man who dared invade her privacy paid with his life. Actaeon, a hunter who spied Artemis bathing at her favorite stream, was turned into a stag and killed by his own hounds. To the Greeks, "virginal" meant whole unto oneself, and Artemis needed no lover, husband, or child to feel complete, as did Aphrodite, Hera, or Demeter. She dealt harshly with anyone who failed to honor her, banishing her nymph Callisto after Zeus seduced her. To a king who made harvest-time offerings to Demeter and Dionysus but not her, Artemis sent a monstrous boar with eyes of fire to trample the ripening crops.

As the hunter, Artemis is often seen with a stag or hunting dog by her side. Her gifts to humankind included wild game for food, necessary for life before Demeter provided the art of agriculture, but woe to anyone who hunts pregnant or young animals or kills creatures needlessly. As protector of wild animals, she ensures the survival of all species. The bear, particularly the mother bear fiercely protecting her cubs, is a symbol of Artemis. Young girls who entered her service were called "she-bears."

Truly, Artemis is the embodiment of pure instinct. She personifies natural law itself and as such, she wields a power that is all encompassing and fearsome.

Her domain is the sweep of natural life, from birth and reproduction to death, and her power is that of the wild beasts, not of the seductress like Aphrodite, or partnership like Hera, or the intellect like Athena. Artemis later absorbed the older Roman goddess Diana, the queen of the open sky and the untamed, but it was in even earlier times that her influence reigned supreme. Her temple at Ephesus, in what is now Turkey, was one of the wonders of the ancient world. There, depicted as a many-breasted Mother Goddess attended by virgin priestesses called "bees," she prevailed as the oldest of the Greek goddesses. Artemis, in all her varied forms, is the pure, primitive feminine.

Create a sense of privacy—so typical of Artemis's beloved nature—with warm wood, natural tile, a few treasured artifacts, and patterns of sunlight through delicate verdure.

ARTEMIS IN YOUR DEN

THE SPIRIT OF ARTEMIS HAS LIVED AND STILL LIVES IN MANY ADVENTUROUS, SELF-KNOWING WOMEN, INCLUDING ANNIE OAKLEY, AMELIA EARHART, KAREN BLIXEN (ISAK DINESEN), ANNE MORROW LINDBERGH, JANE GOODALL, MARGARET MEAD, JANE FONDA AS "BARBARELLA," GEORGIA O'KEEFE, KATHARINE HEPBURN, SYLVIA EARLE, VENUS WILLIAMS, XENA, AND SALLY RIDE. USE THESE SYMBOLS AND COLORS TO CALL ON YOUR ARTEMISIAN INTUITION AND INNER FOCUS.

Even as a young child, Artemis knew exactly what she wanted. "Follow your instincts" is a good tenet for her den. Certainly she would approve of this use of the word *den*, with all its connotations of leaf-filled lairs and protection of cubs. But not everyone has the luxury of a separate den, so carve out an area in another room, if need be, and devote it to this goddess. Natural places instill a sense of peace as well as awestruck wonder. There is no reason you can't bring a bit of that sensibility indoors. Borrow from whatever greenscape you see from your window—tendrils of ivy or a gnarled branch or a river rock—and set it inside. If your view is decidedly unnatural, let your intuition and imagination dictate the woodsy realm you create.

To summon Artemis, invite nature into the den in all its variegated wildness. Add a vase of tangled twigs or aromatic silvery artemisia, unrefined containers of rough clay, woven reeds, drilled stones, or unusual wood burls. Make room for a potted tree or other greenery for a private copse. Uplighting through spiky-leafed palms creates swaying tracery on the walls and ceiling. A hand-crafted chair or table of bentwood, cedar twigs, or logs is reminiscent of old hunting lodges and bears the unique stamp of its origins. Weigh down a stack of magazines with a beautiful stone. Tie an assemblage of leaves, stones, and seed pods to a delicate twig for a uniquely artemisian mobile. Float realistic loon decoys across a tabletop. Fill a whimsical plant holder shaped like an elephant or rhinoceros with claw cactus. Candlesticks or wall sconces of elk antlers shed in the seasonal cycle suggest longevity and the Tree of Life as well as Artemis's companion, the stag. Or suspend an unusual staghorn fern low over a table. Give a mounted moose head a place of honor on the wall. Wire votive candleholders to a twisted branch for a forest chandelier. Find a footstool, table, or chair with thick paw, delicate hoof, or claw-and-ball feet to let the spirit of the wild animals creep inside.

THE SYMBOLS OF ADVENTURE

Artemisia—peppery tarragon, lance-shape western sage, silver-leafed wormwood

Bear

Bow and arrows

Dog

Moon—particularly the crescent moon

Stag

THE COLORS OF INTUITION

Earth tones and colors of the deep woods, mountain streams, sun-drenched meadows

Saffron and red—the colors of her tunic

Silver

White—purity

THE HALLMARKS OF INDEPENDENCE

Bees—for her Ephesian priestesses

Daisy

Fir tree

Laurel

Mirror—clarity of self-knowledge

Quail

Roads and harbors

Verbena

Willow

Pale yellow walls and gnarled branches bring in a touch of the wild outdoors. Exotic and personal artifacts hint at adventures in other lands.

The mind I love must still have wild places, a tangled orchard where dark damsons drop in the heavy grass, an overgrown little wood, the chance of a snake or two (real snakes), a pool that nobody's fathomed the depth of——and paths threaded with those little flowers planted by the mind.

—KATHERINE MANSFIELD

This goddess roamed fearlessly through moonlit thickets. Step boldly into color realms you may have been too timid to try. Earth tones are soul calming, but think beyond "brown" and "green" to embrace the full spectrum of the wild. Instead of the ubiquitous off-white, consider the coloring of a newborn fawn, warm umber, or delicate bamboo. Artemis hid from the river god Alpheius by covering herself in mud. Paint walls like silty loam, sunburned terra-cotta, golden sandstone, or glistening clay. Add a woody hue of oak, ash, or gleaming chestnut. Green is the most abundant color in nature and its variety is without limit. Perhaps the shade that moves you recalls a dappled meadow or velvety lichen, the blue-green of pine forests or the bright yellow-green of young shoots, the shade of a mossy glen or deep woods after a thunderstorm. Add candles or essential oils in green scents like bergamot, oakmoss, or lemongrass, and bask in sensory verdure.

It has been said that color has a language all its own and, like the communication of animals, it can be enigmatic. The colors of animals are nearly as numerous as the shades of green or brown in nature: Think of birds, fish, turtles, and snakes. Think of the tawny hide of a camel, or the shining gold-brown of a grizzly bear, a dusty elephant, a glossy blue-black raven, and the muted taupe of a mourning dove. With a bit of thought, you can use Artemis's colors to express your own style in powerful and subtle ways.

Watery blue and glossy foliage create a peaceful nook to contemplate the journeys suggested in a beckoning waterway.

EVOKING ARTEMIS IN THE DEN

- The girls of the village of Karyai danced to Artemis with baskets of live reeds on their heads. Fill a rough pot with long-bladed rye grass in honor of the goddess.

- Cover your floor with matting in natural fibers like coir, jute, sisal, or rush.

- Fill an antique vase made of horn and silver with delicate white primroses.

- Framed naturalists' sketches depict nature's beauty in every leaf, seed, petal, and stem.

- Add an ivy or fern wallpaper border around the top of the room.

- Pile pinecones and evergreen boughs in a giant wooden bowl and perfume the air with Artemis's outdoors.

- Use natural containers of bamboo canes, twigs, and basketry for magazines and other storage.

- Hang a sheer curtain panel stitched with open-topped sheer pockets. Slide a different dried flower, leaf, or seed pod into each one. Change your selections with the seasons.

A voyage to a destination, wherever it may be,
Is also a voyage inside oneself.

—LAURENS VAN DER POST

A few carefully chosen objects
gathered on a shelf suggest
Artemis's presence and an
individual style.

If the sight of the blue skies fills you with joy, if a blade of grass springing up in the fields has power to move you, if the simple things of nature have a message that you understand, rejoice, for your soul is alive.

—ELEANORA DUSE

ABOVE: Verdant hues, sunset walls, and chairs like plush green tussocks envelop you in Artemis's hidden glade. A painting pays homage to the hunter's faithful dogs.

OPPOSITE: Just a few touches—a faux animal print pillow, flowers, silvery table or lamp, and bird sculpture—are all that is necessary to invite Artemis into your den.

Artemis prowled the oak wood as free and unfettered as the wild animals. Although she shared the quality of strength with the other goddesses, she possessed an untamable individuality. She knew her own nature and cared nothing for the whims or concerns of others.

Develop the look of this room from your own sense of self. Here is a space that announces who you are, where you came from, and where you are going. Here are objects that resonate at the very core of your being, things that speak to your truth and clarity of purpose. Come here to define your boundaries, reflect, and feed your inner strength. Don't be swayed by others' opinions of your choices. Exercise your intuition.

Perhaps there is a favorite animal whose quality of strength, stamina, or pride you admire. You can bring that creature's spirit into your den through artwork, photographs, colors, or pattern. Animal motifs on a Central American mola or Malaysian ikat, African carving, or Peruvian embroidery can help you contemplate the characteristics you value. Choose colors you respond to viscerally, objects that speak to your soul. Some will recall emotions, others memories, but they are all unique to you. Let your individuality sweep through the room like a gust through a mountain gorge. You can follow a known path or take the one that is barely a path at all, that is covered over with brambles and previously unnoticed. Artemis trusted her instincts and listened to her intuition. Don't feel constrained by a particular period or style. Let nature's spontaneity engulf you.

Artemis's spirit can be found in a tabletop as round as the moon, a mirror frame carved in leafy arpeggios, and pure white tones. Vintage prints remember her protection of roads and harbors in ancient times.

When the moon shone, Artemis was present,
and the beasts and plants would dance.

—CARL KERÉNYI

Green glass filters light as if through forest bowers, an appropriate setting for found treasures and a collection of floral printed cards.

Take inspiration from nature's infinite variation and subtle shadings. Granite, leaves, pinecones, nuts, birds' eggs, feathers, fur, and bone offer ideas for color and pattern. Try new ways to incorporate their spotted, streaked, and knobby quirks into your den, such as light fixtures like twigs or upholstery imitating lustrous fur. Animal patterns can be as loud as zebra stripes or as subtle as a quail camouflaged in prairie grass. Cover a chair in a faux leopard print or snakeskin. Make pillows or rugs out of fake fur or the real thing, using old fur coats or sheepskins. Draw on the nobility of the beasts with a small sculpture of a bear or stag. Pay homage to Artemis's faithful hunting hounds. Hang a print or painting of a wild wood or hunting scene.

Cover a wall with handmade paper flecked with bits of grass or flowers, slubby rush paper, or even brown kraft paper you paint or print with leaf shapes. Wipe on layers of colored paint for a rough-hewn look, or splatter different shades of cream, gray, and taupe to mimic a bird's speckled eggs. A more ambitious project might involve a faux finish of weathered wood or striated stone, or even a tromp l'oeil fantasy of an enchanted forest from a fairy tale. Wallpaper embossed with rich William Morris greenery or delicate sedge, fern motifs on curtain fabrics or leaf patterns on carpets add to the lushness of Artemis's room.

Everywhere you look, Artemis gives you ideas in the pulsing vibrancy of nature: Watch the interplay of light and shadow over tall grass, raindrops splattering on slate, moonlight tracery on rough bark, sunlight streaming through bowers, multihued oak leaves in your favorite park. A large piece of smooth-edged glass on a tabletop becomes an ever-changing display of nature's wonders when you press leaves or flowers beneath its weight. Leave a book of beautiful botanical prints or Audubon's exquisite birds open on a table. Open to a different page now and then and reflect on nature's impossible beauty.

Draw ideas from a shimmering herd of black-and-white zebras, the molten red dirt of the Australian outback, or rippling prairie grass. Play on the shapes of leaves—lance, oval, triangular, serrated. Answer the call of the wild with imitation python, ocelot, crocodile, or sable. Animals depend upon their keen sense of smell to provide them with a full picture of their surroundings, which their eyes may not see. Scents conjure vivid memories, remind us of people, and return us to remembered places. Add tones of sandalwood, silver fir needle, or fragrant orange blossom, sacred to Artemis, in your den.

The moon and its mystery are closely associated with Artemis; she moved confidently by moonlight in the darkest of woodlands, her intuition as bright as the waxing moon in an ebony sky. You can see the crescent moon echoed in her silver bow as well as the diadem in her hair. Nature's palette changes completely in moonlight. Experiment with these more mysterious, subtle hues of shadow. Capture its elusive lutescence in lighting. Use crescent moon shapes and motifs.

In nature, nothing clashes. Animal hide, assorted woods, and tendrils of blossoms happily coexist where Artemis dwells.

There are unknown forces within nature; when we give ourselves wholly to her, . . . she leads them to us; she shows us those forms which our watching eyes do not see.

—AUGUST RODIN

Near her temple at Nemi, south of Rome, the round moon-like lake was called "Diana's mirror." Like the moon, a mirror reflects light. Hang a round mirror in the den to reflect the unfaltering light of Artemis's inner truth. Lustrous silver represents Artemis's purity as well as her lunar connection. A silvery lamp, vase, or candlestick glints like wisdom in an earth-toned room.

Artemis is the embodiment of an active, athletic life. She asked Zeus for a short hunting tunic, rather than the long garments worn by the other goddesses, so that she might run unhindered. Lithe and nimble, she roamed freely over the mountaintops with her nymphs and hunting dogs. You needn't take up archery, nor even be athletically inclined, to understand Artemis's sensibility. Take aim with your "arrows" of desires and deeds. Release those arrows as you express your individuality. Find an outdoor activity you enjoy or, if you tend to tamer pursuits, admire the physical and sporting attainments of others through books, prints,

photographs, or sporting memorabilia. Award yourself a flea-market trophy, and fill it with laurel branches or cheerful daisies, plants sacred to Artemis.

Let items that reflect your personal predilections convey the essence of this room and lift it beyond mere utility. Display photographs of your travels to exotic places, whether a continent away or in the next town. Add pictures or artifacts redolent of adventures you plan to have and feed your artemisian spirit. Turn over a new leaf. Collect your found objects and souvenirs here, whatever denotes the life you love or the life you want. Let this room help you cultivate the mind of a young girl. To her, as to Artemis, every day is new and overflowing with potential. She doesn't worry about what others think or expect of her. Her spirit is independent, individual, and untamed. Nature has taken millennia to achieve its splendor. Your Artemis-inspired den is worth some time and thought. Let your imagination run wild, literally.

In this charming gaming room, souvenirs and exotic artifacts from the world over celebrate the independent goddess' adventurous spirit. Make your own declaration of independence when decorating your Artemis-inspired space.

ATHENA
GODDESS OF WISDOM, CIVILIZATION & THE ARTS

ATHENA, LIKE APHRODITE, MATERIALIZED FULLY FORMED, BUT NOT ON A SCALLOP SHELL LIKE THE GODDESS OF LOVE, RATHER FROM THE HEAD OF HER FATHER. METIS, WHOSE NAME MEANS "WISE COUNSEL," WARNED ZEUS THAT THE CHILD OF THEIR UNION WOULD SOME DAY OVERTHROW HIM.

Zeus, assuming the child would be a boy, promptly swallowed the pregnant goddess. Later he developed such a headache that he asked Prometheus to cleave his forehead to relieve his discomfort. Out sprang Athena in a shower of gold, resplendent in gleaming armor, brandishing a spear and emitting a fearsome war cry that shook Mount Olympus. Immediately she won Zeus's favor—she was without question her father's daughter, and some say his equal. Only to her did he reveal the secret hiding place of his thunderbolts. Only to Athena did he lend his magnificent aegis, a snake-fringed goatskin with the terrifying image of serpent-haired Medusa on its breast.

Gray-eyed Athena, whose name literally means the "mind of god," was the most powerful of the Greek goddesses. A virgin with both masculine and feminine characteristics, she required no husband or companion. Males were her colleagues, not her lovers. Strong and dignified, this goddess inspired awe among the other gods as well as among mortals, and she remained above the scandals and petty grievances that colored the exploits of other deities.

Although often clothed in the accoutrements of war and possibly derived from a Mycenean war goddess, Athena is not warlike. Instead, she represents a just and compassionate strategist, mediator, and protector. Patriotic defense rather than aggressive attack is her métier. Resourceful, astute, and wise, she championed many heroes in their exploits. With her guidance, Perseus slew the terrible Medusa, Bellerophon captured and rode the winged Pegasus, Odysseus returned safely to reclaim his home and his wife, Hercules succeeded in his labors, Achilles prevailed against his enemies, and the Argonauts captured the Golden Fleece. Athena helped the Greek soldiers build the Trojan Horse and eventually win the Trojan War.

In earlier times, Athena was a household deity who ruled over domestic crafts and the family. Later, her attributes embraced the Roman Minerva, patron of artisans. The invention of the ship, the potter's wheel, the plow, the flute, music, the domestic arts (such as weaving, spinning, and cooking), and such crafts as carpentry and metalwork are all accredited to Athena. As counterpart to Artemis, Athena helped humans

Bold architectural elements ingeniously define this Athenian office. The way you house your books speaks volumes about you. The same goes for the colorful details—the brightly patterned textiles and whimsical artifacts—that make a workplace comfortable.

tame wild Nature; her bridle and plow controlled beasts for riding and agricultural work.

Unlike Artemis, who seeks solitude in wild places, the worldly Athena thrives in the city and the bustle of the marketplace. Her domain also includes art, drama, and literature, as well as philosophy, mathematics, political institutions, and law—the very hallmarks of civilization. She remains calm and focused in the midst of turmoil and brave in the face of danger. Courageous, loyal, and brilliant, the beautiful Athena knows how to apply her knowledge in practical and useful ways.

If you want anything said, ask a man. If you want anything done, ask a woman.

—MARGARET THATCHER

ATHENA IN YOUR OFFICE

WOMEN WHO HAVE EXEMPLIFIED ATHENIAN FOCUS AND ACCOMPLISHMENT INCLUDE JOAN OF ARC, QUEEN ELIZABETH I, SUSAN B. ANTHONY, ELEANOR ROOSEVELT, KATHARINE HEPBURN, COCO CHANEL, MARGARET THATCHER, GLORIA STEINEM, SANDRA DAY O'CONNOR, JANE FONDA, DIANE SAWYER, OPRAH WINFREY, MADELINE ALBRIGHT, MARTHA STEWART, FAITH POPCORN, AND ERIN BROCKOVICH. BRING ATHENA INTO YOUR OWN INTELLECTUAL AND CREATIVE ENDEAVORS BY USING THE COLORS, SYMBOLS, AND HALLMARKS OF THIS WISE AND CLEAR-THINKING GODDESS.

There is no better place to attend to the affairs of the mind than in the office of Athena, because she stands for focused attention and clarity of thought. Here is where you stockpile books and reference materials—your mental arsenal—for ideas and fact checking. Draw on her logic and reasoning as you approach the design of your office: First, know what you'll use the space for, how often, and what kind of equipment and materials you'll need, then execute your battle plan.

Whether your home office is in a separate building or a nook under the staircase, you can bring Athena's sensibilities to bear, because she has the imagination to make the most of whatever opportunity presents itself. If you can't devote an entire room to an office, a guest room or rarely used dining room can serve double duty. Define the space with shelves, a folding screen, fabric panels hung ceiling to floor, or big potted plants. If you need a spot only for occasional paperwork, repurpose a landing, a corner, the odd space under the attic eaves, or even a large closet. With the modern array of furniture elements that stack, modify, and connect, you're sure to find the perfect ones for your purpose.

Choose furniture that suits the scale of the space, the work to be done, and your temperament. Although a plank atop a couple of sawhorses may be functionally adequate, Athena appreciates good craftsmanship. A beautiful work surface and chair add ceremony and dignity to a place in which you spend a significant amount of time. The desk—whether wood, a smooth-edged slab of glass, leather topped, or laminate—should be a pleasure to sit at and to use. Oak is strong and beautiful, both Athenian qualities. Pair an old farm table with a sleek modern chair, blonde wood and blue laminate, or metal and baroque. Pay homage to the warrior Athena with a shield-back chair. Find a flea-market bookstand and give a prominent place to your dictionary, because this goddess is always interested in words.

THE SYMBOLS OF INTELLECT

Crow

Crystal

Flute, trumpet, music

Loom—productivity, strategy, intricacy of thought

Olive—nourishment, victory, peace, well-being, honor

Owl—wisdom, patience, discernment

Serpent

Thunderbolt—flashes of inspiration, power, realization, ideas

THE COLORS OF CREATIVITY

Blue—imagination, truth

Gray

Olive green

Orange—communication

Turquoise—insight

Yellow—wisdom, power, illumination

THE HALLMARKS OF POWER

Goat (Remember: Her aegis was a goatskin.)

Gold, bronze, and other metals

Horse

Mulberry

Oak

Shield—protection

> *When people keep telling you that you can't do a thing, you kind of like to try it.*
>
> —MARGARET CHASE SMITH

Use natural textures to temper the severity of large, smooth surfaces. Experiment with containers made of woven grass, Shaker wood, colorful cardboard, rattan, papier-mâché, or powder-coated metal for papers, office supplies, or magazines. You can make creative use of architectural salvage: Cabinetry from 19th-century apothecary, hardware, or feed-and-seed stores, complete with drawers and compartments, adds an interesting twist to the concept of storage. Trunks, vintage suitcases, and fabric-covered shoeboxes and hatboxes can find new life storing papers and supplies. Choose decorative stone or ceramic vessels or interesting boxes to hold paper clips and pens. Soften the walls and floor with attractive wall hangings, rugs, and live plants. Orange stimulates conversation. If it's too garish for your taste, tone it down to russet or peach, or add an orange accent with a pillow or a vase of bright dahlias. An office can be all work and still have room for the personal touches of beautiful objects and fragrance. The perfume of the hyacinth is said to help one focus, whereas mint and rosemary are supposed to aid memory and mental keenness. Don't worry about traditional strictures of "masculine" and "feminine." Athena possessed characteristics of both, and you can combine their elements in your office to great effect. Dark walnut or mahogany, painted wood, floral wallpaper, tailored upholstery, metal, glass, leather—if it's well made, it suits your purpose, and you like it, Athena would approve.

Depending on your work requirements, an airy nook that blends into the kitchen cabinetry may be all the office you need. A spacious workroom offers the luxury of spreading out projects, as well as harmoniously combining materials and styles, from a modern acrylic coffee table to an elaborate console.

*Every life is a Great Work, with all the richness of its gifts
and the wealth of its possibilities.*

—CARLY FIORINA

EVOKING ATHENA
IN THE OFFICE

- Look to Athena for help in keeping your wits in emotional situations. Just as she prevented Achilles from killing Agamemnon in anger, call on this goddess to replace the heat of emotion with reasoned judgment.

- Experiment with new ways to strengthen your mental focus: take a class, meditate, try tai chi or yoga.

- Enjoy a cup of tea infused with the sweet, applelike scent of chamomile to enhance your dedication and relieve stress.

- Athena is said to have invented music, the most mathematical of arts. Provide for its enjoyment in your workspace, while you're working or during breaks.

- Honor the "goddess of a thousand works" by trying an art or craft—carve, dance, sing, draw, write, paint, or do needlepoint. Find satisfaction in your accomplishments.

- Choose colors of mustard or periwinkle and scents of lily of the valley and rosemary to enhance mental keenness.

- Place a reproduction bust of Athena or vase with her image on your desk and draw on her strength, resolve, and inspiration while you work.

A utilitarian, eclectic, yet serene, accumulation of textures and objects make an office that is as individual as its owner and uniquely suited to the business at hand.

Athena would have relished the computer age, with all its gadgetry and impact on every endeavor, from the arts to science and math. And she'd have welcomed the realms opened by the Internet, with its instantaneous access to information and lightning-fast communication around the globe. A computer in a rolltop desk may seem incongruous, but Athena wouldn't mind the juxtaposition. Sleek custom-designed cabinets or an antique armoire modified for office use make stylish and clever adaptations for high-tech equipment. Even the most nondescript electronics can be enlivened by an elegant desktop or sculptural shelves.

Athena is ruled by her head, not her heart. She stands for learning and intellectual pursuits of all kinds and has no time for the romantic dalliances of Aphrodite. Although intellect and reasoning are often characterized as "cold," you can warm them up with patterned paper or textured fabrics. Colorwash, rag, or sponge-paint the walls to resemble weathered stone, wood, paper, or fabric. Architecture falls under this goddess' domain, with its combination of precision, mathematics, science, and beauty. Add classically inspired molding, columns, or a pediment to a room or doorway for a note of dignified grace. Place a potted violet on your desk to connote wisdom.

Athena is closely associated with her father, Zeus, and she was unquestionably his favorite. She herself appeared as a mentor and guide to many heroes on their mythic journeys. Your workspace would be an appropriate place to pay homage to your father or a mentor with a photograph or memento, and to reflect on their wisdom and counsel.

Crafts and handiwork were of special importance to Athena. She taught cooking and weaving to Pandora, the first woman. She taught craftsmen how to make chariots of bronze. In one story, Arachne, an exceptionally skilled weaver, challenged Athena to a contest at the loom. The boastful girl hoped to trick the goddess into making a mistake by creating an impossibly beautiful tapestry depicting the Greek pantheon in scandalous poses. When Athena saw it, she tore the masterpiece to shreds and beat the poor girl, who hung herself in shame. The goddess relented and let Arachne live—as a spider so that she might spend her days spinning and weaving.

Athena's loom is an apt metaphor for productivity and intricacy of thought. Weave her inspiration through your own life. If you're fortunate enough to work at home, you needn't be hindered by the cubicle maze of the corporate workplace. You may not weave, knit, or make pots yourself, but you can still appreciate and use the fruits of others' artistry. Add depth and texture with a hand-crafted bowl, petit point–covered chair, carved table, or decoupaged box. You'll see new details every time you look at it. Keep a favorite small sculpture or framed drawing close by, and note how it changes in lamplight and daylight. If you play a musical instrument, make room for it here. If not, it's never too late to learn. Cover a bulletin board with old pieces of sheet music, pages from a secondhand book of poetry, vintage or new postcards of far-off places, fabric, or wallpaper. Every summer Athena's statue was washed in the sea and dressed anew in cloth woven by the city's best craftswomen, so stand an old dressmaker's form in the corner, and drape it as the mood fits. Line the shelves with literature, old favorites as well as soon-to-be favorites. Invest in a finely wrought timepiece.

If we are to achieve a richer culture, rich in contrasting values, we must recognize the whole gamut of human potentialities. We must weave a social fabric in which each diverse human gift will find a fitting place.

—MARGARET MEAD

More is more when it comes to invoking the power and wisdom of the goddesses.

Imagination is more weighty than fact.

—THOMAS MOORE

Athena was often called the "gray-eyed" or "owl-eyed" goddess. Owls lived in her temple on the Acropolis and, it was believed, protected Greek soldiers in battle. Symbol of wisdom and signifier of victory, the owl also adorned the country's silver coins. The Greeks believed that the owl had a magical inner light that enabled it to see in the dark. Call on this bird of prey's powers to hunt down those elusive ideas that scurry in the corners of your imagination. You can find owl motifs in artwork or fabrics, boxes, paperweights, sculpture, or prints. Neutral needn't mean mousy. Be inspired by muted tones of gray and brown that blend into the background like an owl against rough bark. Feathery warm taupe forms a quiet backdrop for polished metal, a vase of tulips, or colorful carpet.

Athena illuminated those she protected by clarifying their thoughts or quite literally lighting their way along a dangerous path. Her insight and intelligence pierced doubt and ignorance like a beam of light in darkness. Free from the sickly cast of industrial fluorescent lighting, you can illuminate your office in any way that pleases you, provided your work is adequately lit. Make optimum use of daylight, if you have it: After all, it's calming to look out a window and rest the eyes away from paperwork or a computer screen. Experiment with ambient lighting spots, table lamps, and floor lamps. Lighting that is flexible—that can be turned to reflect off the ceiling or focus down on a task—lets you adapt it to suit your mood and the job. Mirrors enhance existing light. Brass lamps gleam like Athena's golden armor. Yellow stands for qualities of wisdom, intuition, and power, and its creamy glow on walls is pleasing.

An office can be personal and decorative without being fussy. Athena's touch can be found in such details as the neoclassical chair, brass lamp, flowers, and treasures interspersed among the many books.

Just as appetite comes by eating,
so work brings inspiration.

—IGOR STRAVINSKY

Athena was the only goddess permitted to use Zeus's mighty thunderbolts. When you're working on a project, call on this goddess for those lightning-swift flashes of inspiration that strike like bolts out of the blue. Lighting symbolizes power as well as ideas and quickness of mind. Mimic their zigzag form in patterns on upholstery or curtains. Fling yourself into a project with all your effort, like Athena taking the reins of Diomedes' chariot and leaping into battle against the Trojans.

Anything that stimulates your imagination and creativity is appropriate in this space. John Keats wrote one of the most beautiful poems in the English language while contemplating the figures on a Grecian urn. Who knows where your next spark will originate? Don't relegate your desk to a dark corner. Position it near a window with an inspiring view. If you haven't a view, then hang a painting or a map. Surround yourself with an eclectic assortment of objects. Keep close by books and periodicals full of timely and timeworn ideas that offer new insights every time you peruse them. If you're happy in your surroundings, ideas will flow.

Athena applied her intuition in practical and useful ways. She invented the olive tree, certainly an inspired creation, and so won the patronage of Athens. Branches of the olive, a sacred symbol of peace and honor, make a fitting wreath for Athena's room. Stems of aromatic angelica are said to foster inspiration. Keep the equipment and supplies for work or crafts ready at hand for when that creative spark ignites. Throw a decorative shawl or quilt over your desk rather than tidying it all up, and be prepared when inspiration next strikes.

Reign over your office space in a lovely chair festooned with a pastoral scene, sitting at a simple yet elegant desk lit by queenly sconces.

ELY [LOUR REIL] IT IS NEVER TOO LAT

Even the mightiest heroes of Greek legend felt their courage falter in the face of terrible monsters and insurmountable obstacles. In those times, Athena allayed their dread and gave them heart. She replaced their anger with reason and their fear with determination. Make a place for pictures, quotes, or other reminders of your heroes, whomever they may be. Athena protected the brave—love had nothing to do with it. In one tale, she helped Perseus slay Medusa, the terrible Gorgon who turned to stone any man who looked upon her face. The goddess gave him her polished shield so that he would see only Medusa's reflection as he cut off her head. Call on Athena's strength to face your doubts or stumbling blocks. Find or make a mask, bust, or face that represents your fears and hang it in your office. When you behold its image in a mirror or in a polished metal bowl, you'll see those fears reduced to a pale reflection, with no power over you. When thwarted by doubts, listen for Athena's whisper of encouragement.

You gain strength, courage, and confidence by every experience in which you really stop to look fear in the face. . . . You must do the thing which you think you cannot do.

—ELEANOR ROOSEVELT

Gold leaf, antiquities, classical entablature, and a frieze of quotations carry out the old-world theme of this contemplative workspace—a room to welcome muses as well as musings.

A ship in port is safe, but that is not what ships are for.
Sail out to sea and do new things.

—GRACE HOPPER

Athena bestowed mastery over wind and water when she invented the ship. Like the wind, she breathed direction and will into her heroes when they had none. Ships stir romantic notions of freedom and adventure. Contemplate a model ship, or a maritime painting, and dream of your journeys to come. As the special patron of Odysseus, Athena guided him on his journeys and helped him return safely home. Stir your wanderlust with an oversized atlas, globe, or map. Antiques come with a history; select an object with a story attached—yours or someone else's—to inspirit your flights of fancy. Objects from other cultures kindle interest in faraway places. Under her aegis (and indeed the phrase originates with her magic cloak), a woman can travel freely in realms once closed to her—in the workplace and the world. With Athena by your side, nothing seems impossible if your spirit is resolute. Let your voyage of self-discovery, like that of Odysseus, lead you home again.

At first glance, this office says "traditional," with its leather chair, ormolu decorations, and antiquarian tomes. But the details indicate a well-used and well-loved space—the worn wood and tile, the assorted boxes and containers of interesting shapes and materials. Artwork, flowers, and daylight add to its pleasing mien.

I am independent!
I live alone and I love to work.

—MARY CASSATT

I am like a vine putting out graceful shoots, My blossoms bear the fruit of glory and wealth. Approach me, you who desire me, And take your fill of my fruits.

—PAULA GUNN ALLEN

DEMETER
GODDESS OF THE HARVEST AND FERTILITY

DEMETER PRESIDED OVER ALL GROWING THINGS AND THE FRUITFULNESS OF AGRICULTURE. THE ROMANS KNEW HER AS CERES, WHOSE NAME ECHOES TODAY WITHIN THE WORD *CEREAL*.

In mythology, she's the sister of Zeus, Poseidon, Hades, Hestia, and Hera, and the granddaughter of Gaea, the earth herself. But Demeter is best known as the devoted mother whose grief was inconsolable when Hades abducted her daughter to his underworld kingdom. Indeed, she is so closely tied to Persephone, her daughter with Zeus, that some say they're but two aspects of the same goddess.

One day, the legend goes, Persephone was picking flowers in a field. When she reached for a beautiful narcissus, the earth cracked open and Hades, driving an ebony chariot drawn by midnight-blue steeds, seized her. Persephone cried out, but it was too late. When Demeter heard the faint cry, she felt a stab of pain in her heart, and she left Olympus to find her daughter.

For 9 days, the grief-stricken goddess wandered the earth disguised as a mortal, asking after her beloved child. In her anguish, Demeter rent her blue and green mourning cloak into pieces, which turned into cornflowers. She would not eat, drink, or wash. No one claimed any knowledge of Persephone's fate until on the tenth day Helios revealed that Zeus had allowed Hades to carry off his niece.

Later, as Demeter sat weeping by a well in the town of Eleusis, the daughters of the local king invited her to their home. There the queen welcomed the stranger and bid her stay as nursemaid to her baby son. Demeter treated the child as her own and sought to make him immortal by placing him in the fire while the others slept. One night the queen saw what she was doing and screamed in terror, breaking the spell. Demeter angrily revealed the splendor of her true identity and decreed that the people must build a grand temple to her. When it was finished, she mourned the loss of her daughter there for a year.

As the goddess grieved, nothing grew and famine wracked the earth. The other gods and goddesses, denied their offerings and sacrifices, tried to convince Demeter to return to Olympus. Finally, Zeus dispatched Hermes to tell the dark lord he must return Persephone to her mother. Had she eaten nothing while in the

underworld, Persephone might have remained with her mother always. But Hades slipped a pomegranate seed into her mouth before she departed, dooming her to return to the sunless realm for a third of every year. During those months, Demeter plunged the earth into cold and gloom. In the spring and summer, however, when Persephone was with her mother, the goddess allowed the full abundance of flowers, fruits, and vegetables to cover the earth.

The story then describes how Demeter revealed the life-sustaining secrets of agriculture to Triptolemos, a hero of Eleusis, who took them to all peoples of the earth. She also divulged the sacred rites to be performed at her temple. For hundreds of years, people traveled from far and wide to honor the grain goddess in the Eleusinian Mysteries, rituals that lasted 9 days,

the length of time she searched for her daughter. They offered the first fruits of their harvests to Demeter and participated in ceremonies so secret that their details haven't been unearthed to this day.

In art, Demeter is often seen proffering a sheaf of wheat or "corn," a general term for grain in ancient times, symbolizing all cultivated food. Sometimes she's pictured carrying torches as she searches the darkness for her daughter. To the ancient Greeks, her worship was highly practical, because through her kindness, crops emerged each year. Within her resonates the seasonal cycle—winter's death of growing things and spring's regeneration of them. Unlike the notions of love, creativity, and partnership that preoccupy other goddesses, her domain is nothing less than the continuation of life itself.

DEMETER IN YOUR KITCHEN

EVERY ERA PRODUCES WOMEN WHO ARE STRONG AND NURTURING, WHO EMBRACE "FAMILY"—WHETHER THEIR OWN KIN, THEIR COUNTRY, OR ALL OF HUMANKIND. THESE INCLUDE THE VIRGIN MARY, FLORENCE NIGHTINGALE, "MARMEE" IN *LITTLE WOMEN*, GOLDA MEIR, ROSE KENNEDY, JUNE CLEAVER, MOTHER TERESA, JACQUELINE KENNEDY ONASSIS, DORIS DAY, AUDREY HEPBURN, AND PRINCESS DIANA. USE THESE SYMBOLS OF DEMETER TO HONOR THE NURTURER IN YOU.

Anything that makes you think of nurturing and mothering in its most general sense pertains to Demeter, for her kitchen is warm and welcoming. Her realm encompasses the products of the tilled soil, but this space feeds the soul as well as the body. The kitchen needn't be merely a workroom for the daily chore of cooking: Instead, make it a place you want to linger in over coffee or Saturday breakfast. If your kitchen is dark, brighten it with light-colored tiles, paint, or fabrics. Hide an uninteresting floor with colorful cotton rugs or natural jute mats. If you have more ambitious plans for the room, consider the warm, durable surface of a wood floor, or perhaps a lively pattern in linoleum or tile.

Without sunlight and rain, there would be no agriculture. Large windows, glass doors, and skylights let in copious amounts of natural light and provide a view of the weather in all its moods. Fill a window with glass shelves and potted flowers instead of shades or curtains. Or use a sunny spot for a small indoor herb garden, practical as well as decorative.

Demeter is a tranquil goddess, patient and egoless. Her concern focuses on the well-being of others. Leave ideas of wealth, status, and worldly achievements in Athena's office. Keep glamour for Aphrodite's bedroom. Candles stand for the torches Demeter carried as she searched for her daughter. Pillars with fragrances like pumpkin spice, sugar cookies, or herbs add a homey touch, even when you don't feel like cooking. Or, simmer a pot of apple cider with cinnamon sticks and lemon peel. Myrtle is sacred to Demeter. In fact, 16th-century ladies used its sweet herbaceous tone in skin creams. Keep some scented lotion or soap near the sink, or imbue your kitchen with warmed essential oils of myrtle, bay, and ginger.

THE SYMBOLS OF TRANSFORMATION

Cornflowers

Crane

Mint

Ox

Pig

Pinecones

Wheat

THE COLORS OF NURTURING

Blue and green—hope and fertility; the colors of Demeter's cloak

Gold

Poppy

Warm colors of ripening crops, fertile earth

THE HALLMARKS OF ABUNDANCE

Basketry

Copper

Cornucopia

Fruits and grains

Livestock

Sickle and plow

Although "country" can devolve into kitschy, at its core it is utilitarian and undoctored simplicity. A kitchen can be modern and convenient yet retain an aura of tradition. Plain useful tools for food preparation, such as wooden spoons, can be stored in a stoneware crock or hung on a rack, as pleasing to look at as they are to hold. Cover a wall with thin wood slats in a trellis pattern painted to contrast with the walls. The functional grid can hold pots, ladles, recipes, or photographs. Tuck in a small bouquet of dried herbs and flowers. Display antique biscuit and cake tins or cookie cutters—they're shapely and useful, should you be inspired to bake something. Perhaps you have a collection of rolling pins or family china. Don't save them for special occasions, but use their pattern and color to add life to the room. Find teapots or canisters in the bright hues of fruits or vegetables or shaped like one of her motifs. Copper is associated with this goddess. Hang your gleaming cookware where you can admire its beauty, instead of hiding it away.

If some wizard would like to make me a present, let him give me a bottle filled with the voices of that kitchen, the ha ha ha and fire whispering, a bottle brimming with its buttery sugary bakery smells.

—TRUMAN CAPOTE

A sunny nook for breakfast fits close by counter space. Hanging pots, a favorite collection of transferware, and vanilla walls add to a kitchen's welcoming feel.

We have our summers of sunny pleasure and our winter of discontent, our springtimes of renewal and our autumns of necessary decay. We are essentially rhythmic, musical.

—THOMAS MOORE

The homey gleam of copper pots and pans and the warm comfort of woven baskets and wooden spoons promise good food and good company to those lucky enough to find themselves in this Demeter-inspired kitchen.

EVOKING DEMETER IN THE KITCHEN

- Demeter is a homebody, not a news watcher. Save worldly concerns for other rooms: Put the television and serious books in Athena's office or Artemis's den. Try not to think about career or hobbies here (unless your hobby is cooking).

- One of Demeter's symbols is wheat. Display a small ornament of woven wheat in remembrance of the goddess. Bake some bread. The push and pull of kneading is therapeutic and the smell of baking bread will infuse the entire house with the essence of life and love.

- As part of the Eleusinian Mysteries, the initiates drank barley water and mint, the only nourishment Demeter would take before her daughter was returned to her. Toast the goddess with a cup of mint tea or a refreshing tonic of fruit juice garnished with mint.

- Make your refrigerator a paean to children—yours or those of friends. Use colorful magnets shaped like fruits and flowers to display their photographs and art class masterpieces.

- Keep a well-stocked cookie jar in the shape of a pig, sacred to Demeter.

- Appreciate the simple visual qualities of a bowl of bright oranges and lemons, a wire basket of brown eggs, or a vase of just-picked flowers.

- Invoke Demeter's spirit by appreciating the abundance and variety of her gifts. Try new foods and recipes with ingredients and spices you've never had. Use the freshest ingredients you can find.

All-white dinnerware makes a bold and elegant display when not hidden behind closed cabinets. The white and wood tones form a muted backdrop for the vibrancy of Demeter's gifts.

The Demeter myth celebrates seasonal transformation. Respond to her changing emotions by changing the fruit, flower, color, or motif details of your kitchen according to winter, spring, summer, and fall. Cast a warm glow in winter darkness with candles, just as Demeter lit her path during her search. Ceremonies in her honor begin on September 22. Tie a large sheaf of wheat with a beautiful ribbon, and set it atop coppery leaves for an autumnal centerpiece. Traditionally, soap was made in the spring from lye and cooking tallow. Use generous blocks of natural vegetable soap tinged with fruit essences. Receive the sweet gifts of spring as Persephone's return: birdsong, warm breezes, crocuses, and asparagus. A beautiful bowl or basket of shiny eggplants and tomatoes, earthy potatoes and carrots, and the fresh green of string beans and unshucked corn needs no other embellishment to welcome summer. Stencil bright zinnia patterns around the window frame. Arrange flowers or potted live plants according to the seasons: tulips and daffodils in the spring; poppies, sweet peas, and cornflowers in the summer; strawflowers and forget-me-nots in the fall; snowdrops and firethorn in the winter.

No other room connotes transformation so obviously as the kitchen, for here is where fresh ingredients metamorphose into food for sustenance and pleasure. Using preparation and serving pieces you love and enjoy enhances the delight in the end result. Pottery or bone china, when openly displayed, needs little other adornment. Individual hand-painted or whimsically shaped pieces merit special placement on the wall or on a high shelf near the ceiling. Nothing is more transformative than food itself, which, once eaten, nourishes the body. Select implements, containers, pots, and pans with the care due to the important task of cooking food.

Of all the goddesses, Demeter is the nurturer, the one prepared to care for children or any person or animal suffering from hunger, cold, or want. Healers, doctors, and humanitarians, as well as mothers, display the sensibilities of this beneficent goddess. Her kitchen isn't all hard edges and steel—instead it incorporates some softness and rounded edges in a room that is calming and peaceful.

Demeter's myth is the earliest known story of the relationship between a mother and daughter—one of the most complex relationships of all. Within her story are all the hopes and dreams held by any mother for her child or by anyone for a person or cause dear to the heart. The kitchen has traditionally been the place of women's work. Although that is no longer necessarily true, Demeter encourages connections with the women in our families. Give a place of honor to a great-grandmother's photograph or a gift from an aunt. Use a shelf or wall to honor any women you admire or learned from with photographs, artwork, or objects. Frame a photograph of your mother at your current age and reflect on how her life differed from yours. Decorate a twig or wheat wreath with small photographs of grandmothers and children. Buy a pretty family tree to fill in and hang in the kitchen. The connection with past generations reinforces a sense of continuity.

Feel like a kid again. Invite nieces, nephews, or neighborhood children over for an afternoon cookie-baking extravaganza. It provides an excuse to stock up on cookie cutters in festive animal shapes and an assortment of bright canvas aprons. Hera might balk at the disarray, but Demeter wouldn't mind. Try some time-worn recipes handed down through generations. There's a reason why macaroni and cheese and grandmother's meat loaf are called "comfort food."

Demeter's palette encompasses all the hues of agriculture and the seasons. Confine your imagination only to the colors of her life-sustaining crops, and you'll have more shades than you can use in a lifetime. A rich color harvest can be found in mustard, tangerine, cardamom, papaya, corn, peas, lime, spinach, bell pepper, radish, artichokes, pistachio, turmeric, tomato, cherry, strawberry, peach, mango, cayenne, cocoa, potatoes, carob, and shallots. Surely some of these tints suit your taste. Use them to pickle a cupboard, color a counter, enamel the trim, or lacquer a table.

And so our mothers and grandmothers have. . .handed on the creative spark, the seed of the flower they themselves never hoped to see——or like a sealed letter they could not plainly read.

—ALICE WALKER

The calming blues and greens of Demeter's cloak, the richness of wood, and the vitality of living plants create a kitchen that is a balm to the spirit.

Where long shadows of the wind
had rolled, Green wheat was yielding to the
change assigned, And as by some vast magic
undivined, The world was turning slowly
into gold.

—EDWIN ARLINGTON ROBINSON

Spicy foods speed up the metabolism. If your kitchen is bland, heat it up with ristras of dried ancho peppers and braids of garlic hanging from the ceiling, or a habañero print on the curtains. Line the backsplash with hand-painted tiles of blazing sunflowers or swaths of sizzling pink and orange. Paint walls the rich yellow-orange of hot chili oil or the color of curry, jalapeños, or cilantro. Warm up the trim in candied ginger, cinnamon, or garam masala, and feel your blood race. Add a dash of cayenne color to a teapot, mugs, or plates for a kitchen pick-me-up. As in cooking, spices go beyond nourishment—they're pure pleasure.

You can enrich the room without gaining a pound. Smooth the walls the color of creamery butter, egg yolks, cheesecake, or flan. Add countertops or cupboards in hues of caramel, praline, or croissants. Brighten windows with blinds in lemon meringue, tapioca, or crème anglaise. Chill out with cool tones of mint, cantaloupe, and escarole, or wallpaper scattered with oranges or lemons. Try preparing a color menu for your kitchen, depending on the season and your tastes. Serve up eggplant, vanilla, and sage, or lettuce, blueberry, and cream, if you feel so inclined. Or, pick a cuisine and let it determine your color "palate": African black bean, okra, and mango; Mexican mole, tortillas, and salsa; or Greek olive leaves, rice, and lemon. The results will look good enough to eat!

Folk art and potted herbs lend a nostalgic touch to this light, airy space, where casual dining takes on an intimate elegance that is oh so Demeter.

Vegetables are a physical pleasure to buy and clean and prepare and then cook and serve forth. I love their color, and odors, and the feel of them.

—M.F.K. FISHER

Cooking is as much about touch and feel as it is about taste and smell. If your kitchen is all smooth artificial surfaces, find ways to incorporate some natural textures, such as wood, slate, stone, rattan, tile, or textiles. This can be as simple as adding a wooden cutting board, colorful cotton dishtowels, and an earthenware pot to hold cooking implements, or as ambitious as adding granite countertops or cork flooring. Rustic textures of terra-cotta, brick, weathered wood and metal, or pottery add dimension to the dinnerware, furniture, walls, and other details. Filter sunlight through textured shades of rough burlap. Intermingle modern cabinetry with an older piece, such as an antique corner cabinet, pie safe, or vintage baker's rack.

Inspiring patterns are everywhere in Demeter's realm, from the checkerboard of plowed fields, to the pale and dark streaks on a watermelon, to the yellow rows of kernels in an ear of corn. They can be as subtle as the violet and cream on an asparagus stem or as assertive as a tree studded with brilliant sweet oranges. Rather than hiding your staples away, fill clear glass canisters with layers of red and green lentils, pinto and black beans, or tricolor rotini. Marinated olives and herb-infused oils come in bottles and jars too pretty to keep in a cupboard. Display your dinnerware and serving pieces on open shelving, the pots and pans on hooks, the ladles, spoons, and whisks in a redware jar. They'll add texture and be near at hand.

The ancient Greeks appreciated the flavors and restorative effects of herbs. Plant an herb garden outdoors, in a window box, or as a live centerpiece. The results are decorative, aromatic, and flavorful.

An assortment of textures intermingles delightfully in basketry, marble, iron, rattan, wood, jars of preserved fruits, and playful tiles that mimic the china.

A wreath of herb twigs is beautiful, functional, and fragrant, although you can also tie bunches of dried herbs with raffia and hang them from the ceiling. Frame horticultural prints, or find wallpaper or dinnerware with delicate herb patterns.

Beautiful baskets were an integral part of the Eleusinian Mysteries. Even though they can be decorative in their own right simply hung from the ceiling, you can put them to good use hanging from pegs to store dish towels or utensils; resting on counters to hold fruits, vegetables, or bread; or sitting beside tables and chairs for cookbooks and magazines.

Sarah Bernhardt was once presented with a giant bouquet of vegetables artfully carved to resemble real flowers. However, you can find simpler ways to incorporate vegetables into your kitchen's diet. Tiles, wallpaper, and fabrics festooned with favorite vegetables are available. Use wallpaper scraps to cover switch plates. Hollow out small gourds and pumpkins to use as vases or as molds to make harvest-themed candles. Make a collage of fruit or vegetable prints. Liven up meals with festive majolica shaped like leaves, cabbages, or fruits. Hang a vegetable alphabet poster or an assortment of colorful California fruit crate labels.

The kitchen is a place to cook food, yes, but it's also a space for sharing meals with family or entertaining friends, a room that invites others to sit a while, have some tea, and share a moment. In Demeter's kitchen there is always the promise of plenty—a piece of fruit, a slice of bread and butter, or a more substantial meal together, for her spirit is generous and her heart full of warmth. Her son with Iasion was Ploutus, god of wealth, and the true spirit of "wealth" resounds through her associations with family, abundance, and friends. Few things symbolize Demeter's largesse quite like a cornucopia overflowing with fruits, vegetables, and flowers. Use the images of her abundance to draw her spirit into your kitchen.

Demeter's gift of agriculture meant that people no longer had to depend on hunting for food, and they settled in communities. Historically, the preparation of food was a communal activity, and cooking is still one way that people come together. Large work surfaces and island units, where several people can help prepare food, encourage connection and community. Whether laminate, granite, or rough-hewn farm table, open spaces invite cooperation and conviviality. Cooking is as much theater as work—let others enjoy the show.

A kitchen that connects living and cooking spaces encourages conversation. A dining table does double duty as a work surface, allowing many people to participate.

Season of mist and mellow fruitfulness,
Close bosom friend of the maturing sun;
Conspiring with him how to load and bless
With fruit the vines that round the thatch-eves run

—JOHN KEATS

Demeter helped humankind domesticate animals for food and work. Give a nod to her gift with a folk art painting of a fat sheep or hen, a collage of 19th-century state fair postcards, or a country scene to remember that food really doesn't originate as frozen cardboard boxes. Pigs are sacred to this goddess. Their motifs appear on ceramic tiles, cookie jars, or flea-market figurines. Cows and other farm animals show up in primitive paintings, advertising art, printed fabrics, and old spongeware creamers. March a wallpaper border of handsome roosters near the ceiling.

Demeter was highly honored in ancient times, because she stood for all that was life-affirming. She demanded that offerings to her be in their natural state, so supplicants left unspun wool, honeycombs, grain, and grapes on her altar. Use the beauty of her unmilled wheat and just-plucked fruits to grace your kitchen. Then play Demeter in grand style, and invite your family and friends to partake in a feast fit for a goddess.

With the spirit of Demeter infusing your kitchen, you'll find yourself happily singing at the sink while you prepare simple feasts for friends and family alike.

HERA

GODDESS OF MARRIAGE

QUEEN OF OLYMPUS, THE DIGNIFIED AND STATELY HERA RULED OVER MARRIAGE, BUT THAT WAS A COMPARATIVELY RECENT RESPONSIBILITY FOR THIS GODDESS. FAR OLDER WAS HER WORSHIP AS ONE OF THE ORIGINAL MOTHER-GODDESSES LATER FRAGMENTED INTO THE GREEK PANTHEON.

Hera, whose name means "lady," ruled the feminine spirit, the cycles of a woman's life, and childbirth. She had no need of a companion, and thus one understands her vexation when forced into marriage with the sky-god Zeus.

In Greek myth, Hera was a daughter of Rhea and Cronos. Although some make her Zeus's twin, others say that she helped her mother save Zeus from the fate of their siblings. Cronos, worried that one of his progeny would overthrow him, swallowed Hestia, Demeter, Poseidon, and Hades as soon as they were born. With Zeus, Rhea tricked Cronos into swallowing a stone wrapped in swaddling clothes, while Hera hid the baby in Crete.

Hera was raised by the Seasons on the island of Euboea, "the good cow country," and she's sometimes called the cow-eyed goddess. One story claims she chose her youngest brother to be her husband as soon as he was born; another describes Zeus's persistence as he wooed the unwilling goddess. Finally, disguised as a storm-tattered cuckoo, he fell into her lap. Hera took pity on the poor bird and held him close to her. Suddenly Zeus regained his true form and would have forced his way on her, but she struggled until he agreed to marry her. She couldn't have anticipated the turmoil this union would cause her.

Many thought Hera's beauty to be unequaled by any other goddess. Each year she bathed in a spring at Cathanos to renew her virginity. She was also known to borrow Aphrodite's magic belt to make herself irresistible to her husband. Hera was never unfaithful to Zeus, so it pained her to watch his endless infidelities. With tempers of Olympian proportions— once Zeus strung Hera up by her wrists, with her feet weighted with anvils—others often suffered during their disagreements. She vented her anger on his mistresses, sending a gadfly to torment Io, burning Semele alive, and turning Callisto into a bear.

Hera's relationships with her children drew scant attention, as her focus remained squarely on the doings of her husband. Her daughter, Hebe, cup-bearer to the gods, later married Hercules. But two of her children give an indication of the fiery, combative nature of Hera's marriage: Ares, god of war, and Hephaestus, god of fire. It's told that she produced Hephaestus from her thigh, out of spite, when Zeus brought forth Athena from his forehead. She never cared much for the lame blacksmith, and threw him into the sea for others to raise.

Preoccupied as she was with Zeus and his mistresses, and hounding Hercules on his 12 labors, Hera had little time for the inventions and accomplishments attributed to other goddesses, although she won the rule of Argos over Poseidon. In Roman times, her myth mingled with that of Juno, protector of women and married life, and so acquired a more benign aspect than just that of possessive wife. But there is no question she was highly revered and devoutly worshipped, perhaps not least because she seemed so fallible, so human. In her union with Zeus, Hera could be subdued but she was never dominated. At times she embarked on solitary journeys to the dark ends of the earth, and there rediscovered her own inner strength. Only then did she accept Zeus fully, and calm her jealous heart.

HERA IN YOUR DINING ROOM

HERA'S REGAL BEARING BRINGS TO MIND MANY DIGNIFIED, DETERMINED WOMEN WITH EQUALLY IMPORTANT PARTNERS: ABIGAIL ADAMS, QUEEN VICTORIA, EVA PERON, JANE WYMAN IN *FALCON CREST*, HILLARY RODHAM CLINTON, PRINCESS GRACE, NANCY REAGAN, AND LAURA BUSH. CHOOSE AMONG THESE SYMBOLS, COLORS, AND HALLMARKS TO ADD REFINEMENT TO YOUR DINING ROOM.

Hera's proud bearing clearly marks her as queen of the gods. Dedicate your dining room to her as a place for the enjoyment of companions, conversation, and cuisine. Picture Hera turning up her regal nose at the idea of an energy bar as adequate repast. The gods dined on ambrosia, but you can enjoy humbler fare in a room touched by this majestic goddess. You don't even need a special occasion to turn a meal into a dignified and ceremonial event. Slow the pace. Eat with chopsticks. Dine by candlelight. Drink beverages from small tea bowls. Use your best china. If your dining room shares quarters with other activities or if you have an eat-in kitchen, you can visually and mentally separate the eating of meals from the rest of daily life: Banish the television or hide it in an armoire when it's not in use, and use a lavishly decorated folding screen between the dining area and other areas.

Any dining room devoted to this goddess is the antithesis of demure. Borrow from the stately homes of Europe, and let architectural detail impart an air of splendor to this important space. Reshape a square doorway into an arch. Clad the walls in paneling or framed panels of noble wallpaper. Try wainscoting or a frieze fit for a queen, an embossed dado, or a chair rail with old-world grace and new-world practicality. Apply gold- or silver-leaf to the trim, and see how it glows softly in candlelight. Encircle the room with a plate rail or display shelf, and show off your porcelain. Arrange your wedding silver on a hutch or marble-topped console. The Victorians provided for the comfort of dinner guests with individual footstools: Pamper your guests underfoot with a dark maple floor, aristocratic tile, or thick oriental rug. Stencil a border of gold chevrons around the edge of the floor. Fill an urn with marigolds, which symbolize power.

THE SYMBOLS OF PARTNERSHIP

Fig tree

Golden apple

Goose—love, vigilance

Immortelle

Interlocking rings

Ivy—symbol of marriage and fidelity

Orange blossom

Quince—lifelong fidelity

THE COLORS OF ROYALTY

Deep red

Gold—perfection

Ivory—stability

Rich purple—power

Royal blue

THE HALLMARKS OF MAJESTY

Crown

Cuckoo

Marigolds—power

Peacock—pride, beauty, immortality

Quartz crystal—confidence

Throne

For one human being to love another; that is perhaps the most difficult of all our tasks....

—RAINER MARIA RILKE

Give windows the royal treatment with a handsome cornice, shirred swags, softly draped cascades, or tailored jabots. Brocade draperies glow opulently in soft light. Tie them back to glass wall brackets with gold ropes and ceramic tassels. Anoint the walls in a color that, like Hera, can hold its own. Deep burgundy or carmine stimulates conversation and appetite and flatters candlelit complexions with a rosy glow. Or replace a few of the lightbulbs with colored lights if you don't want to commit to red walls. Imperial sconces warm the walls with dramatic indirect light. Splurge on an impossibly glorious chandelier dancing with crystals or one that looks piped out of Royal icing. Replace regular light switches with dimmers so you can fit the mood to the occasion.

Here you preside over family and social gatherings, whether for 2 or 20. Small or large, round or square, choose a dining table that suits the room, your needs, and your budget. A suite of matched furniture adds formality, but you don't need a full complement of mahogany to present a courtly appearance. Top an Ionic pedestal with a round of clear glass. Unify mismatched chairs with comfortable cushions, fine upholstery, or stylish slipcovers. When the table isn't in use for meals, lay out a grand bowl of fruit, cachepots of plants or flowers, or tapers in golden candlesticks. Highlight an emerald vase of crimson roses. Cluster star-shaped royal bluebells in a cut-glass candy dish. Float candles in a silver bowl. Scatter tiny lights like diamonds among pieces of lead crystal to sparkle like a queen's ransom.

Hera's magnificent statue on Euboea sat on a gold and ivory throne, a symbol of stability and unity. Once, Hephaestus made an exquisite throne for his mother. When she sat on it, invisible chains bound her tightly and the chair flew into the air. The blacksmith released her only after he was promised Aphrodite's hand in marriage. Just like Hera, you deserve a throne. Whether it's rococo revival or gothic romantic, a secondhand find embellished with gilding and brocade is fit for the empress of the domicile.

Bedecked in quince silk and damask and bedizened in candlelight and gold, this dining room is prepared for a royal audience—or an intimate dinner with a few close friends.

Smooth columns and soft drapery swags distinguish the dining area from the living room. Large windows, elegant sconces, and candelabra, all crowned by a chandelier that Hephaestus might have crafted, provide a medley of lighting choices to suit any dining occasion.

Juno Regina was the protectress of Rome and is often pictured wearing a crown. Deep crown molding is aristocratic and aptly named, because it draws the eye upward, literally crowning the walls. Scepter-shaped sconces and a chandelier like Hera's diadem complete the genteel effect.

Dress your room as if it were to be presented at court, with ruffled, tiered, or cloud shades, billowing taffeta swags, satin curtains, or drapes the sumptuous velvet of a queen's cloak. Add a bit of faux ermine for good measure. Give the windows a soigné silhouette with an Empire or Queen Ann valance, lambrequins, or a wooden cornice stenciled with golden crowns. Long

ago, nobility selected the iris, or fleur-de-lis, to represent faith, wisdom, and valor. Iris was Hera's messenger and slept beneath her bed to await her mistress' bidding. This regal motif adds grace to fabrics, furniture, carpets, and wallpaper.

If your family name has a coat of arms, have it worked in enamel or needlepoint and unveil it here. If not, borrow the lions rampant, griffins, and shields to use as motifs in Hera's room. Paper the walls with gilded royal monograms. Your dining room can be magnificent without being palatial. Create a centerpiece of purple crown vetch, irises, and creamy white queen-of-the-meadow, and hold court.

- Asterion grew on the riverbanks in Euboea. Weave a garland offering for Hera, just as the ancients did.

- Celebrate March 1 in honor of this goddess, when Roman husbands gave presents to their wives and prayed for their health. Women dressed in their finest, exchanged gifts, and entertained family and friends at banquets.

- Dedicate to Hera a corner garden in your yard, and plant violet queens, crown daisies, peacock plant, and bridal wreath.

- Treat your dining experience with honor and ceremony. Invoke the protective, powerful spirit of Hera with a few words before a meal. Take the time to savor proudly cooked and graciously presented food.

- Paint the ceiling a soft silver and trim the drapes with golden bullion fringe, in honor of Juno Moneta, guardian of the Roman mint.

- Borrow from the great palaces of Europe: Faux paint marble over the wood, alabaster blocks over the walls, and inlays of malachite on the sideboard drawers.

- Pay homage to Juno Viriplaca, settler of arguments between spouses, with a beautiful meal and a centerpiece of gardenia, lavender, and morning glory, symbols of harmony.

The purpose of life as a woman is to ascend to the throne and rule with heart.

—MARIANNE WILLIAMSON

Though you have never possessed me
I have belonged to you since the beginning of time

—MING LOY

Llewellyn

All gods and goddesses attended the wedding of Hera and Zeus, resplendent with gifts and good wishes. Gaea presented them with a tree bearing the golden apples of the Hesperides. Find beautiful apple motifs on fabrics or carpets, hang a painting of the succulent fruit on the wall, or fill a Limoges bowl with the real thing. Many cultures celebrate marriage by drinking from a common cup. Inaugurate your own custom with a delicate chalice or cut-glass goblets, and store them where they can be seen.

The wedding night of Zeus and Hera lasted 300 years. Celebrate the enduring loves in your life by conferring a place for heirlooms and portraits in Hera's dining room. Here, where kith and kin break bread together, such objects of continuity foster a sense of family and history. Crocuses adorned the marriage bed of this goddess. Cultivate bulbs of gold, bronze, and purple in an exquisite shallow bowl atop your harvest table.

Of all the goddesses, Hera sought completion and partnership with a devoted companion. It certainly wasn't a concern of Aphrodite with her many lovers, or Demeter with her preoccupation with her daughter, or of the virgin goddesses who had no need of men. Despite Zeus's many indiscretions, Hera remained true to him. In her honor, paint the walls the color of quince, a symbol of lasting fidelity. Fill a glass vase with boughs of hawthorn or sprays of lilies, both associated with marriage. The month of June is named for this goddess and remains the favorite month for weddings. Garnish a corner with a small orange tree in a terra-cotta pot, and enjoy the fragrant blossoms that Hera twined in her hair. In festivals that celebrated her marriage, Hera's statue was washed and dressed in bridal raiment. Sheer fitted slipcovers as diaphanous as bridal veils wisp delicately over side chairs.

Hera was the only Olympian goddess whose stature equaled her husband's. Consider an egalitarian round table, whether for a few or a dozen. A demilune table is perfect for an intimate luncheon for two. Choose decorations of interlocking rings, symbols of steadfast love.

Marriage is the symbolic recognition of our identity—
two aspects of the same being.

—JOSEPH CAMPBELL

Like a queen, a dining room should have various outfits for different social occasions, from simple to couture. Experiment with neutrals and jewel tones. Layer lace over linen, a silk scarf over simple cotton, a boldly patterned floor cloth over bare wood. Add flounces, ruffles, bows, or tassels to your table's wardrobe, if you like. Unfurl a runner of gold net over brocade, and scatter with fall leaves. Spill a river of amethyst taffeta down the length of gleaming walnut. Weave ribbons into a covering of your own design. Toss a Turkish kilim over the dining surface; it won't show spots and your guests will feel as though they're dining in a castle. Dress your table with inexpensive ethnic shawls, painted canvas, colored paper, gorgeous sheets, or nubbly burlap. Hera is so beautiful—she looks good in anything. A small chest of drawers makes decorous storage for linens and flatware, with space on top for pottery or candelabra.

Think of the flatware, plates, and other items you use at mealtime as the jewelry adorning Hera's table. Layer glass plates and goblets in sapphire, emerald, and ruby. Mix and match old flatware in patterns like "Fidelis," "Empress," or "Crown Baroque." Use dishes in solid colors to complement old china in patterns like "Royal Majesty" or "Peacock." Add a touch of formality to your eating experience with cloth napkins and napkin rings. Make your own out of luxurious remnants and beads, wire, costume jewelry, and other found objects. Nestle warm dinner rolls in a basket lined with a bit of tapestry cloth. Resurrect such forgotten niceties as knife rests, place cards, and individual salt cellars complete with their impossibly tiny spoons. Make lavish placemats out of damask and metallic braid, and add glamour to everyday dining.

You may not entertain royalty, but you can entertain friends royally. Pull out all the stops with sparkling emerald and ruby glassware, silver, and Sèvres. If you don't live in a palace, paint one on the walls and pretend.

The Horai opened and closed the gates for Hera as they guarded the entrance to Olympus. Formalize the passage into your dining area by framing the entry with a pediment and classical columns, pilasters, or molding, or replicate the effect of a Victorian rope portiere with cord or beads to heighten the sense of occasion. Paint clouds on the ceiling like those that veiled the craggy peaks of Mount Olympus.

On February 1, the Romans celebrated Juno Sospita. Blindfolded virgins brought cakes made of barley to a snake that lived in a sacred grove. If the snake accepted the offerings, the year would bring healthy children and plentiful crops. A 100-headed serpent, Ladon, protected Hera's golden apples, the wedding gift from Gaea. Pay homage to Hera's sacred snakes with serpentine patterns in fabric, sinewy swirls in woodwork, or coiled snake motifs in furniture.

Long before Hera's marriage to Zeus, she was revered as the goddess of birth and death, spring and fall. Her imposing statue at Euboea held a cuckoo, symbol of spring, and a pomegranate, symbol of autumn. Venerate the cyclical renewal associated with this goddess, and transform your dining area with colors and flowers suited to the changing seasons.

A garden view, bright fabrics and dishes, and flowers help celebrate summer's return.

Each pang of jealousy offers a way to enter more profoundly into ripened life and open-hearted love.

—THOMAS MOORE

When Zeus turned his lover Io into a heifer to hide her from Hera's wrath, the goddess guarded the cow with the monster Argus so Zeus could not reach her. Zeus then bade Hermes to lull the monster to sleep with his lyre, and when its 100 eyes were closed, he killed it. Hera honored the beast's faithful service by removing his eyes and putting these "jewels bright as stars" on the tail of the peacock. The bird is an apt symbol for this goddess, because both embody beauty and pride. A pair of the birds drew Hera's chariot. To the ancients they stood for immortality, because it was believed their flesh never decayed.

Feathers have long been used as decorative objects in the home, because they connote good fortune and prosperity. Assemble a pleasing vase full of plumage instead of flowers. Show off a ravishing tapestry or artwork of peacocks in the dining room, or cover the walls with a wallpaper pattern of pavonine feathers.

Mimic a lacy pinnate look with a large kentia palm.

Vanity comes to mind when considering both Hera and the peacock. Woe to the woman who presumed to compare her attributes to the charms of this goddess. For such an offense she drove Proteus's daughters mad, turned Gerana into a crane, and sent Orion's wife Side to the underworld. Iridescent turquoise, purple, and gold fabrics shimmer in trembling candlelight. Decoupage colorful bird prints on the wall. Hang a lustrous azure fan, spread open like the tail of a proudly strutting peacock.

Geese were also sacred to Hera. They warned the Romans of an impending attack by the Gauls, and another warned of an earthquake. Juno Moneta, "the warner," protected the Roman mint and gave us our word for money. Fold cloth napkins in clever shapes of birds or flower blossoms. Cover the chairs in avian-themed fabric or richly figured needlepoint.

Love comes from years
of breathing
skin to skin
tangled in each other's dreams
—MARY MACKEY

Hera's mythology encompassed the three phases of womanhood. She was Parthenia, the maiden; then Teleia, the wife and mother; and finally Theira, the woman alone. This is the same rhythmic, tripartite theme seen in the new, full, and waning moon. Assemble a collection of round moonlike mirrors over a console or sideboard, to reflect candlelight and the glow of silver. Paint the ceiling a softly gleaming silvery gray, like moonlight. The Greeks celebrated Hera in the Heraea. At this festival, women took part in races in a field near Argos, bare-breasted and hair unbound. They raced in groups, according to age, and the three winners wore crowns of olive branches and placed small images of themselves in Hera's shrine. The ancients believed each woman possessed her own inner "juno," celebrated on her birthday. Place a photo or portrait or object that represents you in this room—let your spirit mingle with Hera's. Find motifs of olive branches and commemorate your juno.

When her troubles with Zeus became too much to bear, Hera would wander the earth in solitude, shrouded in darkness. Through her journeys, she came to know her own identity, separate from her husband's. Hera might be gone for months at a time, but she always returned. Make this room one you want to return to—warm, welcoming, beautiful, and personal, redolent of your life and your dearest relationships.

One day, Hera returned to her birthplace to be alone. Zeus pretended he was about to marry a maiden, but Hera discovered that the "maiden" was no more than a wooden statue dressed in robes, a contrivance designed to trick her. From that moment, Zeus no longer had control over her. Hera returned to her throne, secure in the serenity and partnership that were finally hers.

Richly appointed chairs, crisp table linens, gleaming silver, and graceful birds—just right for a romantic tête-à-tête.

HESTIA
GODDESS OF HEARTH AND HOME

AS FUGITIVE AS FLAME, AS EPHEMERAL AS WOOD SMOKE, HESTIA IS THE LEAST TANGIBLE YET MOST PERVASIVE OF THE GREEK GODDESSES. LIKE CURLING VAPOR, SHE PERMEATED EVERY DWELLING AND COMMUNITY IN THE ANCIENT WORLD. NO STATUES OF HER REMAIN, AND SHE'S SELDOM DEPICTED IN ART, BECAUSE SHE'S EMBODIED WITHIN THE LIVING FLAME ITSELF. PLATO TELLS US HER NAME MEANS "THE ESSENCE OF THINGS," FOR HESTIA IS THE WARMTH AT THE VERY CORE OF FAMILY AND SOCIETY.

This most sacred of the Greek goddesses was said to be the firstborn of Cronos and Rhea. Her primacy sparked a saying among the Greeks, "Begin with Hestia," meaning "Begin things at the beginning." Paradoxically, she was the first to be swallowed by her father and the last to be disgorged, making her both their oldest and youngest child.

Like Artemis and Athena, Hestia had no use for men. Although both her brother Poseidon and her nephew Apollo wooed her, Hestia asked of Zeus only that she be allowed to remain a maiden. After Aphrodite's dalliances and the upheaval of Hera's relationship with her husband, Hestia's desire to remain alone comes as something of a relief. Zeus also granted his sister the first and last portions of every sacrifice made to all gods and goddesses, an indication of the high esteem in which she was held. Hestia's Roman counterpart, Vesta, was especially revered and had a public hearth in the city's center. There, six Vestal priestesses tended the fire, garbed in purple-edged white tunics. Each took a vow of chastity and served for a term of 30 years. During their service and for the rest of their lives, the vestal virgins were highly respected and honored; however, breaking the vow meant death.

Unlike the other, often-contentious virgin goddesses, Hestia was mild and dignified, holding herself apart from the squabbles of her fellow Olympians. Described as the most charitable goddess, she relinquished to Dionysus her place on Mount Olympus. She took no interest in wars or adventures, because her place was at the altar, in the very center of every home and town. In the home, she bestowed peace and well-being on its inhabitants and reminded them to be hospitable to travelers and strangers. In public, Hestia abided in the *prytaneion*, the central hearth in each Greek city, where officials greeted important visitors and anyone could find refuge. Her primary place of worship was at Delphi, but in truth, Hestia's temple existed anywhere her fire burned. Stately and reserved, Hestia left the histrionics to her flamboyant siblings and their offspring. In her own quiet way she fostered contemplation, not contention, peace, not strife.

HESTIA IN YOUR LIVING ROOM

MANY WOMEN HAVE EMBODIED HESTIA'S DIGNIFIED AND CHARITABLE NATURE. LIKE HER, THEY DWELL IN THE CENTER OF COMMUNITY AND HOME, WELCOMING FAMILY AND STRANGERS ALIKE INTO THEIR HOMES AND HEARTS. SOME INCLUDE DOLLEY MADISON, GERTRUDE STEIN, MARIAN WRIGHT EDELMAN, MAYA ANGELOU, AND SIOUX LEADER AND MENTOR FAITH SPOTTED EAGLE. SELECT SOME OF THE SYMBOLS, COLORS, AND HALLMARKS OF THIS GODDESS FOR NOTES OF WARMTH AND PEACE IN YOUR LIVING ROOM.

It isn't hard to understand why the ancients considered flame a living being. You feed it and it grows, and like people, pets, plants, or relationships, you must tend to it or it dies. Think of any image from history that depicts a happy home, and invariably it shows a family grouped around the hearth. This image abides even now, in an age when fewer homes have fireplaces and the living room's focal point is likely to be the television.

Virgil said that this goddess was "more easily felt than explained." Similarly, you can fashion a living room where you and your guests feel comfortable, without being able to point at any one particular thing and say that is why. It's a feeling of enveloping warmth that can be achieved with or without an actual hearth, if you call on Hestia. It's her spirit that transforms a house into a home. Family—and familiarity—is what matters most to this goddess, and the design of the room should reflect this sensibility.

Hestia never drew attention to herself, so her living room is neither loud nor ostentatious. Choose colors that are soothing and a sofa that is inviting. Grays and browns are calming. Warm them up with flashes of gold, orange, or red. Add plump pillows, cozy fabrics, and a supply of throws for nestling in front of the fire. She's the "stay-at-home" goddess, but where Hestia is concerned, the phrase has no unfavorable connotations. Her home is a haven and refuge from all of the cares and struggles of the outside world.

The Greeks say that Hestia invented domestic architecture, because all activities in the home radiated from her central hearth. The scale is human, the mood intimate. Here at the heart of the house, pull the chairs close and kindle companionship. Make the most of your fireplace, whether it's terra-cotta, tile, concrete, brick, or stone. If your mantel could use a facelift, your choices are endless. Add drama to undistinguished wood with bold color, or faux paint it to look like marble or stone. Face the firebox with handpainted tiles, tempered glass, or try a copper or mirrored surface to reflect the room's light. Find an antique mantel that suits your room and the scale of your fireplace. It might be ornate or plain, with columns or

THE SYMBOLS OF WARMTH

Fireplace

Flame, candles, torches

Hearth

THE COLORS OF HARMONY

Purple—trim on tunics of vestal virgins

Red, orange, yellow, blue—the colors of a well-tended fire

White—purity, ash

THE HALLMARKS OF HOSPITALITY

Candles

Circles, spirals

Little houses

Mantel

Rounded shapes

Mid pleasures and palaces though we may roam,
Be it ever so humble, there's no place like home.

—JOHN HOWARD PAYNE

Upholstered chairs and ample light
for reading, a comfy couch for
lounging, and a cuddly throw for
snuggling suggest pleasant
evenings spent near a blazing fire.

The fireplace is really the domestic altar, the true rallying point of the household.

—MARY GAY HUMPHREYS

corbels, pilasters or garlands. Remember: What it lacks in inherent decoration you can add yourself.

A mantel, whether a simple floating shelf or something more elaborate, is unsurpassed display space. No matter what your taste, you can hardly go wrong. Try traditional candlesticks and a mirror; a collection of interesting plates, boxes, or other favorite objects; a vase of fresh or dried flowers; a magnificent painting or poster, symmetrical or not—whatever you desire. Compose an arrangement that pleases you, and change it with the seasons, holidays, special occasions, or just because.

In the summer or when the fireplace isn't in use, clean out the ashes and fill the firebox with dried flowers. Disguise the opening with a pretty screen made of fabric, needlework, painted wood, or decoupage.

Hestia can be present in your home even if you don't have a hearth. What things bring you comfort and soothe your soul? Perhaps you have a favorite handwoven rug or needlepoint pillow, a bright window seat flanked by bookshelves, a treasured antique or family heirloom. Enjoy them in this room. Glaze the walls with yellow or color them in tones of ocher or terra-cotta. A dark-colored ceiling makes a room cozier. Shade the lamps with wood veneer, amber glass, or ecru paper for a golden light. Dimmers allow you to brighten lights for projects and reading and then lower them to flickering softness for more intimate gatherings. Curtains add warmth as well as privacy.

Behind the drapes, coppery sheer curtains dance like flames in the sunlight. Replace glass doors with mirrors on cabinets to enhance daylight or heighten the effect of firelight or candlelight. There is something richly satisfying about a fire's reflection in a gleaming wood floor, soft rugs underfoot, and an evening free from responsibilities.

Throughout time and across cultures, the fire has been a place of gathering together for storytelling, music, and conversation. Think of campfires in the Old West, scout camps, or President Franklin Roosevelt's fireside chats. Today, there are even websites called "campfires," devoted to the exchange of stories and recipes. A fire's glow has an indefinable magic, a warmth beyond the mere heat of the flames. Hestia was worshipped as the goddess of the "community of citizens." Her living room is welcoming because she makes guests feel cherished and safe. Not welcoming is a room in which no thread is out of place or where visitors hesitate to leave a shoe imprint in the plush carpet. A room that looks lived in—indeed, is lived in—feels homey. Make this a place where family and friends want to gather. Provide floor cushions for extra seating and tables that are adaptable for games, crafts, coffee, or homework. Keep a nearby stash of puzzles and amusements, photo albums and objects to spark conversation. Cluster comfortable chairs for chatting, and bookshelves and lamps to encourage guests to linger.

EVOKING HESTIA IN THE LIVING ROOM

- In early June, the Romans celebrated the Vestalia, when Vesta's temple was cleaned and barefoot women brought offerings of salt cakes. Clean winter's ash from your fireplace, wash off the stones or tiles, polish the mantel, and drape it with a fresh garland in honor of this goddess.

- Make time and space in your living room for activities your family can do together, such as games, reading, crafts, or homework.

- Celebrate Hestia with flowers and plants like flame nettle, desert candle, flame violet, heart of flame, or flaming sword.

- On March 1, Vesta's fire is renewed. In her honor, light a fragrant candle in a warming scent of clary sage, sandalwood, or frankincense.

- A laurel tree shaded the hearth at Hestia's primary shrine. Hang a fresh laurel wreath on your mantelpiece.

- Sacrifices to Hestia included first fruits, water, oil, and wine. Build a blazing fire in your hearth, and drink a toast of fine wine to the goddess.

- Caring for one's home can be a ritual to Vesta. Don't think of it as drudgery. Methodical cleaning invests you with calm, cleanses the spirit, and fosters joy in your surroundings.

- To "heap coals of fire upon one's head" means to react with kindness and generosity to insult or injury, certainly a worthy Hestian practice.

"Stay" is a charming word in a friend's vocabulary.

—BRONSON ALCOTT

Hang your hat and welcome. A cheerful living room with a bright fire is the perfect restorative for weary travelers.

"Keep the home fires burning" was a popular refrain during World War I. The image fills us with nostalgia, which means "homesickness." Through the ages, the thought of a cheery fire in the hearth has brought comfort to anyone far away from loved ones. Hestia's fire burned constantly for hundreds of years. Odysseus yearned for home, where his wife, Penelope, kept the home fires burning during the long years of his journey. To Hestia, home is a sanctuary from the rest of the world, where we feel protected and loved. Her hearth is the heart of the home.

If a public flame went out in ancient times, it had to be rekindled from scratch, not another flame. The proper tools will keep your home fires burning, but they can be stylish too. You can find andirons that are playful or plain, animal shaped or polished brass. Keep long matches in an attractive container. If you don't have built-in wood storage, stack logs in a handsome willow, hemp, or twig basket, a wrought iron holder, a wooden box, or an antique copper or galvanized tub. Lay in a supply of pinecones, fruitwood kindling, and dried herbs and citrus peel for an aromatic blaze.

Today we bring housewarming gifts to friends who move into a new house, hoping thereby to bestow protection and luck, and helping to transform the dwelling into a home. Hestia's spirit certainly abides in this custom. Give a friend or yourself a small symbolic house to connote Hestia's protection.

Invested with calm, the browns and creams, soft fabrics, buttery leather, and rough stone of this living room invite repose. The oversized coffee table can accommodate books, bridge, or an informal meal.

During their siege of Athens, the Persians put out Hestia's sacred fire. Later, the victorious Athenians rekindled their fire with flame from her temple at Delphi. When the Greeks founded a new city, they took fire from one public hearth and used it to start the flame in the new one, uniting the new with the old. Newly married women started their hearth fires with flame from their mothers' hearths. Today we see remnants of these ancient rituals in the ceremony of the Olympic torch—a flame carried from Greece to light the flame in the host city. Celebrate the presence of Hestia through the ages with traditions and objects passed from one generation of your family to the next. Make a special place for an heirloom in her living room.

Like moths, we're drawn to flame. Its bright dance is mesmerizing and soothing. Don't save candles for holidays; use their seductive glimmer and delicate scent to make any occasion—or no occasion—special. Gather a profusion of tapers (well away from fabrics, pets, and tiny hands) atop or in front of a mirror. Assemble a tableau of fragrant pillars inside the fireplace. Cluster candles inside an antique birdcage. Line a votive verge around the room. Position lighted candles to add drama to sculptures or flowers and animate their shadows. Arrange a medley of candlesticks and holders—brass, glass, marble, ceramic. Don't limit your waxen palette to white or to the one size. Stoke your imagination to its luminous limits. Find elegant candle sconces for your walls. Imitate the look of candles with electric lanterns of pierced metal or beveled glass, or candlestick lamps with chandelier bulbs, or even a chandelier—who says only Hera can have one? Cover the lights with beaded shades to shimmer like flame.

Better to light a candle than to curse the darkness.

—CHINESE PROVERB

Candlesticks, an ornate antique clock, and a mirror add drama to Hestia's living room.

*Call it a clan, call it a network, call it a tribe, call it a family.
Whatever you call it, whoever you are, you need one.*

—JANE HOWARD

Hestia and Demeter were sisters, so it wasn't unusual for them to be depicted seated together. But there is another connection. Demeter presided over food itself, but because food was cooked in the hearth, Hestia's purview included meal preparation. The first morsel of food was always dedicated to her—and Hestia Tamia guarded the food supplies. Bread, too, was baked in the hearth, so this goddess was a patroness of bakers. Roast some chestnuts or pop some popcorn over the fire, and dedicate the food to Hestia. On a chilly winter evening, wrap your dinner plates in a thick dish towel and warm them on a trivet at the hearth. Share a glass of wine and a warm loaf of bread with a dear companion next to the roaring blaze.

The donkey is sacred to Hestia. During celebrations in Hestia's honor, garlands were draped around the necks of the donkeys that turned the millstones. Seasonal garlands look beautiful draped over the mantelpiece. Garland motifs can be found on fabrics and wallpapers as well.

Hestia and Demeter cohabit cozily when the living room, dining area, and kitchen blend together.

There are two ways of spreading light: to be the candle or the mirror that reflects it.
—EDITH WHARTON

Even without a fire, whimsical designs, tile, an eclectic collection of objects, and a hand-painted fire screen keep the focus on the hearth.

There is a saying, "Where your focus is, that is where your energy goes." When we lose focus, so the Greeks believed, we lose touch with Hestia. This calm and stable goddess doesn't like constant change, like a fire that is whipped and snuffed out by the wind. Hestia inhabits the sheltered quiet corners. Hestia, we are told, never moves. We must go to her in order to rekindle and revitalize the spirit. What matters most to her is feeling secure, at home, and at peace.

For millennia, Hestia's *hearth* (from the Latin word for "focus") was the focal point of every home. If you have a hearth, whether massive stone or delicate tile, it quite naturally becomes the focus of the room. Lavish material possessions don't sway this goddess. She's self-assured and centered, always the same.

Fire screens run the gamut from modest to formal, simple screens to elaborate curlicued extravaganzas, glass or metal. Choose your favorite to suit the décor, then substitute another in fabric or wood to cover the opening in warmer seasons.

If your living room doesn't have a hearth, create a focal point with paint color, art work, a large interesting piece of furniture, a window with a great view, a colorful rug, or a cabinet or shelves with a treasured collection of objects. Whatever makes this room the ideal place to gather your thoughts and energy suits Hestia just fine.

Hestia abides in the warm terra-cotta walls, the casual assemblage of paintings, and the companionable grouping of comfortable chairs, ready for talking, reading, or backgammon.

The soul doesn't evolve or grow, it cycles and twists, repeats and reprises, echoing ancient themes common to all human beings. It is always circling home.

—THOMAS MOORE

In Roman times the only round temple was Vesta's. The Greeks thought that the sacred *omphalos* at Delphi was in the center of Greece and the earth. For them, Hestia's flame burned at the very center of the universe.

The circle is the simplest shape, perfect and peaceful. It connotes balance, infinity, and the earth. You and friends encircle a campfire. An embrace encircles you. Circles and spirals suggest warmth and protection without end. Buddhists meditate gazing on mandalas. There is an age-old custom of carrying a newborn around the hearth to welcome the child into the family. Find ways to use rounded shapes in Hestia's living room—fat cozy curves in furniture or fabric motifs, cylinders in columns, candles, lamps, and other details. Wreaths connote happiness and look beautiful over a mantel. In the swirling repetition of shapes is the suggestion of rhythmic cycles of days, seasons, and life itself, pleasing to the eye and a balm to the soul.

Beautiful curves and circle motifs accentuate every inch of this 1903 ladies' drawing room, from the chandelier, delicate plaster work, and mother-of-pearl inlay on the pink marble, down to the graceful andirons, the pinecones on the fender, and carpets—even the back of the firebox can't elude embellishment.

PERSEPHONE
GODDESS OF LIFE, RENEWAL & TRANSFORMATION

PERSEPHONE, THE DAUGHTER OF DEMETER AND ZEUS, EXPERIENCED THE MOST DRAMATIC TRANSFORMATION OF ALL THE GODDESSES. UNLIKE THE EVER-QUEENLY HERA OR THE CONSTANT FLAME OF HESTIA, PERSEPHONE EPITOMIZED THE JOURNEY FROM LIFE TO DEATH, SPRING TO WINTER, AND BACK AGAIN.

As an innocent and beautiful maiden known as Kore, she spent carefree days lovingly protected by her mother. Later, Persephone ruled as the pale queen of the dead beside her husband in his underworld kingdom. Her story, along with that of her mother, came to be celebrated in some of the most sacred and secret rituals in ancient Greece.

It comes as no surprise that Zeus's gloomy brother Hades had no success finding a companion to share his dismal realm. When his niece caught his eye, he sought Zeus's help in obtaining her for his wife. Zeus well knew that Demeter would never consent to such a union for her daughter, and so advised his brother to kidnap Persephone.

One day, the story goes, Persephone was picking flowers with other maidens, including Artemis and Athena, when she spied a beautiful blossom she had never seen before. It was a narcissus, which Gaea had created at Hades' bidding to tempt the girl. Just as Persephone reached for the flower, the earth cracked

open and Hades, in an ebony chariot drawn by midnight-blue steeds, seized her. Persephone cried out, but it was too late, for the earth closed over them and she was borne away to the underworld. Other than Demeter, only Hecate heard the girl's cries, and only Helios, the Sun, saw what had happened.

Demeter's grief was so great that eventually mankind and even the gods themselves felt its effects. Finally, Zeus dispatched Hermes to the underworld to bring Persephone back to her mother. Hades let her go, telling her that should she return to him, "thou shalt rule over all living creatures and shalt have the greatest honor amongst the gods." In her joy, she failed to notice the pomegranate seed that the dark lord slipped into her mouth. Eating that tiny sweet seed, the food of the dead, destined her to return to his realm for one-third of every year.

Each spring, Demeter's happiness at Persephone's return revealed itself in the profusion of flowers, fruits, and grains she caused to sprout. But every winter she

plunged the earth into cold darkness, withholding all green and growing things while her daughter was away. Demeter's story is a familiar one, but Persephone's is more mysterious and subtle. The Persephone who returned to her mother was no longer the childlike maid so abruptly stolen, for she returned as a woman who had known despair and darkness. The goddess grew to accept her fate, and it was said she ruled with grace and compassion. If not duly honored, she could snatch life away, but in the next instant she could breathe life into the tender buds of spring. Hers is a story embracing great joy and great sorrow. Like Persephone, anyone can feel trapped by the desires of others, held captive by unnamed fears. The pale queen can help us plumb the depths of our own psyches, and grow and adapt to events that, unbidden, buffet the soul.

PERSEPHONE IN YOUR GARDEN OR PERSONAL SHRINE

PERSEPHONE'S ESSENCE CAN BE SEEN IN MANY WOMEN WHO ARE SENSITIVE AND PERCEPTIVE, OR WHO SEEM TO HAVE A SYMPATHETIC SENSE OF THE CYCLES OF NATURE. SOME OF THEM INCLUDE LAURA IN *THE GLASS MENAGERIE*, SYLVIA PLATH, SHIRLEY MACLAINE, ISABEL ALLENDE, WHOOPI GOLDBERG IN *GHOST*, MARIANNE WILLIAMSON, ELISABETH KÜBLER-ROSS, AND SISTER HELEN PREJEAN. USE PERSEPHONE'S SYMBOLS TO ENHANCE YOUR OWN CONTEMPLATIVE SPIRIT.

A personal garden or shrine should be a private space away from bustle and routine, providing quiet moments of meditation and stillness amid the whirl of daily life. Persephone's personal shrine can be a window, a shelf, or a niche in the wall. It can be atop a piano or a dresser, a mantel, a section of bookcase, or a small table covered with a beautiful cloth. It can be inside a closet, in a corner with a comfortable chair and potted plants, or on a porch overlooking a flower bed. It can be a small section of the yard with a favorite rock or tree, or a large private garden. Whatever and wherever it is, it should be a place that brings you calm—a place where peacefulness can be celebrated or sadness, such as that felt by Demeter, can be assuaged.

You may not have a yard or space for a garden, but you can still create a sanctuary within your home. Even a windowsill with tendrils of ivy instead of a curtain and light filtered through bits of colored glass can be a place of calm. Select a favorite spot and put in it the objects that hold particular meaning for you. They might include a collage or memory box with photographs, a poem, and some mementos. Hang a mobile made of natural or handmade items to twirl gently in the air. Assemble small objects, candles, artwork, and flowers atop the mantel. Make it as colorful and personal as you like—this is your space. It should be calming not stimulating, enveloping not claustrophobic. The myth of Demeter and Persephone reminds us of the cycles of birth, growth, death, and birth again. For the ancient Greeks, hers was a story of hope. Use her space to imbue your soul with serenity, to reflect, and to rekindle your spirit.

Persephone's garden takes you away from the bright glare of the computer screen and, if possible, away from the hum of traffic. Small or large, it's a meditative space where your concentration focuses on nothing more important than the patterns in mottled bark, swaying grasses, or bright flowers. It might be a small rock garden in a corner of the yard. Strew handfuls of wildflower seeds in a patch of dirt, and see what comes up. If you like, place here a statue, column, or shapely urn—one or two will do, depending on the size of your sanctuary. A welcoming spot for repose

THE SYMBOLS OF TRANSFORMATION

Butterflies

Gate

Mint

Narcissus

Pomegranate

THE COLORS OF SOLITUDE

Blue—mourning in ancient Greece

Garnet

White and black—light and shadow

THE HALLMARKS OF SERENITY

Parsley

Torches, candles, lamps

Two faces or masks

Willow

Sitting silently / Doing nothing,
Spring comes. / And the grass grows by itself.

—OSHO

might be a stone bench, a wrought iron or weathered Adirondack chair, or a settee fashioned of rough logs or twigs that seems to blend into the landscape.

Demeter carried torches as she searched the darkness for her daughter. The simple act of lighting one or a few candles is serene. Add some to your personal shrine. Hang paper or woven rush lanterns from the trees. Line a pathway with luminarias. Persephone shows us that we can weather loss and grief and survive darkness. Let her light your way.

Bring Persephone's vernal spirit indoors. A window box full of lilies of the valley, petunias, and poppies for happiness and hope looks from inside as though you live in the midst of a garden. Make a space in your special sanctuary for plants in pots or hanging in ceramic or wire planters. Contemplate an entire forest in a bonsai tree. Once when Hades pursued Minthe, jealous Persephone turned the nymph into a mint plant. Add a touch of mint to your garden or potted indoors, and enjoy the flowers, aroma, and flavor. Balance the cerebral cares of Athena and the amorous escapades of Aphrodite with the peace that Persephone can bring, for hers is a place to *be* not to *do*.

*Sacred space and sacred time
and something joyous to do is all
we need. Almost anything then
becomes a continuous and
increasing joy.*

—JOSEPH CAMPBELL

*When I go into my garden with a spade and dig a bed,
I feel such an exhilaration and health.*

—RALPH WALDO EMERSON

EVOKING PERSEPHONE IN
THE GARDEN OR SHRINE

⊞ Tune in to your inner voice and perceptions, and learn to trust your intuition. Write down your dreams, or write in a journal.

⊞ Express yourself by painting or sketching in your sanctuary space to uncover emotions and thoughts that lie hidden beneath consciousness. No one else needs to see your efforts.

⊞ Listen to music that moves you deeply.

⊞ Explore a religion or belief system unfamiliar to you.

⊞ In ancient times the Greeks used fragrant mint, rosemary, and myrtle during funerary rites. You can enjoy their scents in your garden or indoors. Besides its culinary and medicinal uses, rosemary stands for remembrance.

⊞ Follow the Roman example and offer a libation to the departed by pouring a glass of wine or honey into the earth.

She walks in beauty, like the night
Of cloudless climes and starry skies;
And all that's best of dark and bright
Meet in her aspect and her eyes

—GEORGE GORDON, LORD BYRON

Persephone, or Kore, was a carefree child, watched over and adored by her mother. Position two masks or small figures or statues facing each other to remember the powerful mother-daughter love between these goddesses. Although her abduction caused great sadness, Persephone's annual return brought happiness and the regeneration of all living things. Share Demeter's joy by nurturing the flowers that tint the early days of spring: daffodils, tulips, crocuses, and lilies of the valley. Add some hollyhock, verbena, and phlox to attract butterflies, themselves symbols of transformation. It's said that you'll have good luck all year if the first butterfly you see in spring is white.

A chariot symbolizes Persephone's journey of transformation. Acknowledge her odyssey with a small wagon or barrow in your garden. To reach the underworld, Persephone had to pass through the adamantine gate guarded by Cerberus, the three-headed dog. A gate symbolizes transition, an entrance to another place, the separation of two worlds. It might be wrought of iron curlicues or fashioned of weathered planks. Perhaps it's an arch dripping with wisteria or a vault of rough boughs tilted together like swordsmen at a royal wedding. Even if your garden is small, a threshold denotes a break between daily routine and quiet private sanctuary.

Persephone's path led her from childhood to the realm of the dead and into queenly adulthood. Let your path—mossy pavers, salvaged bricks, or crunchy gravel—take you on a journey through your garden. Sounds can transport you away from the commonplace. Perhaps your preference is for Asian bells or gentle wind chimes made of bamboo, glass, shells, or slices of stone. Listen for Demeter's sighs through the leaves and the rustle of her cloak as she searches for her child.

The deepest, most mysterious well of soul holds the secret I seek
and cherish: a strong, solid, rooted, creative sense of self.

—THOMAS MOORE

The light of others drowns the deep magic hidden in the profound darkness.

—LUCIAN BLAGA

Persephone was brutally wrenched from her childhood, but the Stygian goddess came to accept her fate, ruling as a merciful queen in a sunless realm. She greeted Hercules as a brother when he came to fetch Cerberus in the last of his 12 labors, and she let Orpheus take his beloved wife back from the dead. As queen of the underworld, Persephone possessed a sacred grove of black poplars and willows. Plant a small copse of willow and yew trees, beautiful expressions of mourning and sorrow, or a cedar tree, denoting strength. Areas of bright shade and deep shadow in your garden are reminders of Persephone's annual journey between the warm nurturing light of Demeter's love and the darkness of Hades' kingdom.

In Greek, *temenos* is a sacred enclosure. The River Styx encircled the underworld nine times. Feel a sense of enclosure in your garden, either with a fence softened with creeping morning glory or honeysuckle, or with a border of stones. Hades owned no property aboveground, but all of the gems and precious metals under the earth were his. Adorn your personal shrine or garden with semiprecious stones, crystals, and flowers bright as jewels: moonstone for intuition, amethyst for spirituality, and daisies for Persephone's youthful innocence.

Cling to the last vestiges of fall before the goddess' departure with autumn crocus, begonias, grape-leaf anemone, or toad lilies. Cherish your garden in the pale cold light while Persephone is away. Skeletal branches, spikey seed pods, and dry grasses etch starkly beautiful patterns against the leaden sky and barren earth. Soon enough, warmth and green will reappear with Persephone's return.

Where Persephone disappeared in the earth, Kyane, the "dark spring," appeared. Let the soothing murmur of water in your shrine or garden float your cares away.

PHOTOGRAPHY CREDITS

Sandy Agrafiotis, 130

Courtesy of All Tiled Up, 6; 30 (top right); 126; 139; 140; 143

Eric Lessing/Art Resource, NY, 34; 52; 123

Giraudon/Art Resource, NY, 24

Réunion des Musées Nationaux/Art Resource, NY, 10; 26; 70

Scala/Art Resource, NY, 88; 106

Tate Gallery, London/Art Resource, NY, 124

Fernando Bengoechea/Franca Speranza, srl, 66; 110; 121

Courtesy of Doris Leslie Blau, Ltd., 21

Guillaume de Laubier, 13; 14; 20; 23; 27; 28; 31; 32; 37; 39; 40; 44; 45; 61;
68; 76; 80; 82; 83; 97; 101; 105

Michael Garland/ Nicholas Walker & Associates, 75

Steve Gross & Susan Daley; 22; 25; 65; 87; 98; 100; 120; 129; 132

Courtesy of Heirloom European Tapestries, Inc., 102

Leo Murphy, 94; 144

Greg Premru, 49; 84; 96

Eric Roth, 15; 16; 17; 18; 19; 30 (bottom left); 33 (bottom left); 43; 46; 47;
50; 57; 58; 69; 72; 79; 90; 109; 113; 114; 117

Tim Street-Porter/www.beateworks.com, 33 (top right); 54; 62; 77; 93; 118;
135; 136

SPECIAL THANKS TO

All Tiled Up
17725 Chatsworth Street
Granada Hills, CA 91344
818-363-2624

Doris Leslie Blau, Ltd.
724 Fifth Avenue
New York, NY 10019
212-586-5511
www.dorisleslieblau.com

Heirloom European Tapestries, Inc.
P.O. Box 539
Dobbins, CA 95935
800-699-6836
www.tapestries-inc.com

Nicholas Walker & Associates
P.O. Box 1426
Crystal Bay, NV 89402
818-503-4555
nickwalker@nwainc.com

ACKNOWLEDGMENTS

A pantheon of talented people contributed to this book. My deepest thanks go to Paula Munier, a wonderful friend and the best editor anyone could have. I can never adequately express my appreciation to her for entrusting me with her brainchild. I relied completely on Betsy Gammons' unerring eye and assured guidance through the book development process. Patricia Paquette's prodigious research skills located some exquisite images. Stacey Follin copyedited the manuscript with a conscientious light hand. And special thanks go to Winnie Prentiss, Jen Hornsby, Kristy Mulkern, Regina Grenier, and all the people at Rockport Publishing who made this book possible.

ABOUT THE AUTHOR

During 25 years in the museum profession, A. Bronwyn Llewellyn has written about topics as wide-ranging as the civil rights movement, midwestern history, and high technology. She holds a Bachelor of Arts in English from William Jewell College in Missouri and a Master of Arts from the Cooperstown Graduate Program in New York. Ms. Llewellyn amuses herself by writing screenplays and cowboy poetry and by creating knitted garments, handmade art books, and jewelry for friends. She lives in the San Francisco Bay Area.